ALSO BY ADAM RICHMAN

America the Edible:
A Hungry History, from
Sea to Dining Sea

Straight Up Tasty

MEALS, MEMORIES, and MOUTHFULS from MY TRAVELS

ADAM RICHMAN

CLARKSON POTTER/PUBLISHERS
NEW YORK

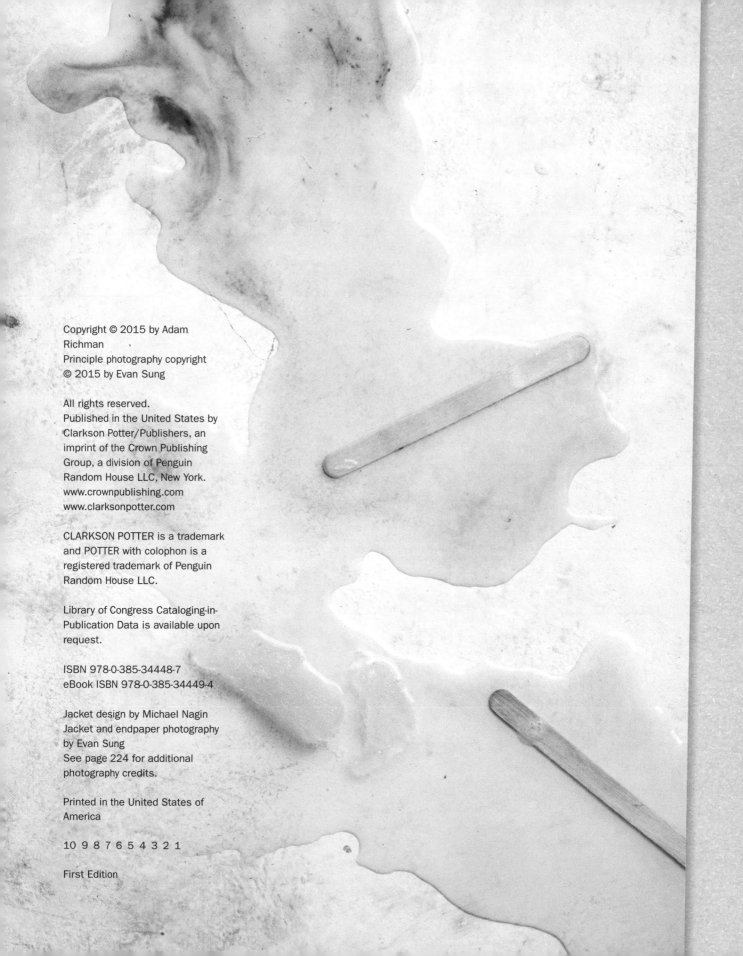

Library of Congress Cataloging-in-Publication Data is available upon request.

ISBN 978-0-385-34448-7
eBook ISBN 978-0-385-34449-4

Jacket design by Michael Nagin
Jacket and endpaper photography by Evan Sung
See page 224 for additional photography credits.

Printed in the United States of America

10 9 8 7 6 5 4 3 2 1

First Edition

If you love to cook,

> this book is for you.

If you love to eat,

> this book is for you.

If you want to learn a few recipes,

> this book is for you.

If you've ever been too intimidated to try cooking,

> this book is for you.

If you are interested in the edible world around us,

> this book is for you.

If you want to search the world fork first for the greatest bites around,

> this book is for you.

If you love to entertain,

> this book is for you.

If you wouldn't mind showing off a little bit,

> this book is for you.

If you think food is deadly serious and not to be approached lightly by the unskilled,

> this book is DEFINITELY NOT for you.

If you're a fan, family, a friend, a foodie, a fine person, a famished person, a food fanatic, or just ready to explore and go from eater to egg beater, consumer to creator. If you love life and tear into it with all the passion for the deliciousness it holds:

> This book is for you.
> This book is for you.
> This book is for you.

INTRODUCTION

So that guy you know for eating the greatest—and craziest— dishes from around the world, he has a cookbook now?

Yup.

He's not eating the food, he's actually making the food?

Yup.

But that guy isn't a chef, right?

Nope.

And that guy doesn't even have a restaurant, right?

Nope.

But he can cook and came up with these recipes himself?

Uh-huh.

And they're good?

You bet your bottom dollar they are.

Okay, now that we've gotten the obvious questions out of the way, let's get down to brass tacks: Why did I write a cookbook, and why is this one different and special and unlike others you may come across?

Well, you'll find the first answer right in the rhetorical questions above. I'm not a chef, and I don't have a restaurant. I am better known for eating than I am for cooking, and I'm more like the folks watching my shows than I am like the cooks I feature. But that's actually the point.

These are recipes I make, that my family makes, that my friends have made. They reflect the flavor combinations, techniques, and ingredients I've picked up on my travels these past few years and all the wonderful and weird meals I have tried, from street food in Ciudad Lanús outside Buenos Aires, to upscale soups

at New Orleans' hottest restaurants. I've been inspired by all kinds of cooks, too, from Berber tribes in the middle of the desert to good ol' boys making barbecue in Georgia, Arkansas, and North Carolina. And you'll see all these influences in the recipes that follow.

This isn't a bible, and it isn't a manual—it's a road map to great eating. In addition to the recipes, you'll discover some fun facts and learn about some great places and amazing dishes to check out when you're on the road yourself. Above all, though, remember this: as with any great road map, detours from the planned route sometimes yield the greatest treasures. If you like a recipe but want to try your own spin or add a super-special ingredient or something from your hometown or personal history—go for it!

Recipes are ever shifting, ever changing, and ever evolving. When choosing the dishes to include in this book, sometimes I reimagined an existing dish; sometimes I just gave you my version of a classic. Some of these recipes I've been making for my family for years and have never changed one iota; others were mere figments of my foodie imagination until I started testing recipes for this book. Some are super easy and comprised entirely of readily available ingredients. With these, the emphasis is on technique and timing. Other recipes are more about flavor nuance and finesse instead of "add stuff to bowl and stir" and may require a little more effort. I humbly submit that the

extra work will be worth your while.

Either way, the focus in *Straight Up Tasty* is on one thing only: **flavor**. Not on American cooking, seasonal cooking, regional cooking, farm to table, or some other arbitrary umbrella used to group food into categories for the ease of librarians and the unimaginative. I believe the best dishes, whether simple or complex, are flavor explosions that make you rethink the edible world we live in, and that's exactly what I've tried to provide here.

While filming around the globe, I'll often turn to the crew that has been with me across many miles and over many months and say, "The pork from this North Carolina barbecue place would be amazing with the tortillas we had in Tampa, the salsa from San Diego, and the pickled onions from Albuquerque." Someone else will say, "No—this pork, the Cuban bread in Tampa, the queso from Santa Barbara, and the homemade pickles from New York, with the sweet potato tots from Charlotte." And on and on it goes.

And, really, why should culture and distance prevent these flavors from combining? Why shouldn't initiative, imagination, and a bit of effort spent on shopping for ingredients yield the flavor wallop we want to give our taste buds? No reason at all! Like the great hip-hop DJs I've always admired, I'm a mix master, creating your mash-up mouthfuls and robust meal remixes. I'm on the ones and twos, the wheels of steel, the pots and pans, the meat and fish.

In this book we are gonna follow rules. We are gonna break rules. You're gonna see a bunch of recipes that are easier than you could have imagined and others that may prompt you to say, "I have to do that, *too*?" But no matter what, I promise you this: you will *love* these dishes. If you have a tongue to taste with, a mind open for exploration, and a spirit that wants to hurl itself out into the flavor void

to see what's out there, you are in for one delicious journey. This is food that we all can make, all can love, and all can appreciate. Getting our *nom nom nom* to the break-a, break-a dawn.

No gimmicks, no fancy equipment or chemicals, and no attitude. Just fun. Just flavor. Just straight up tasty, y'all.

From my kitchen, from my history, to you and yours.

Now let's get this party started . . .

—ADAM RICHMAN

BREAKFAST

ONE OF THE MOST OVERUSED SOUND BITES

in the food world is that breakfast is the most important meal of the day. I'm not saying it's not true—fueling up for the grueling rigors of the day ahead makes total sense. But in the everyday world of regular humans, too often this means dashing out the door and grabbing whatever waffle, muffin, bagel, wrap, or smoothie we come across on our way to work and then mashing it into our face as we dive headlong into our inbox, our morning meetings, our first class of the day. It's a simple fact that, as important as it is, as beloved as it may be, we don't always give breakfast its due. We definitely don't always allow time in our day to prepare breakfast, much less to enjoy it. These recipes, culled from my experiences and my travels, will elevate the classic "Wakey, Wakey—Eggs and Bakey" to something special, something culinarily substantial, something easy to re-create, and something straight-up tasty. Now get up, get out there, and go get 'em, tiger!

WHERE TO GET THE MOST IMPORTANT MEAL OF THE DAY

"Eat breakfast like a king, lunch like a prince, and dinner like a pauper" is an often-heard adage. It's probably more of a lesson about limiting calories late in the day than a comment on the ingredients themselves, but dinner does seem to have a monopoly on all the exquisite, rare, and expensive things with the fancy names, such as chateaubriand, langoustine, bottarga. Even brunch gets caviar and champagne and blinis! Poor breakfast is most commonly associated with humble ingredients such as oats, eggs, and bread. Fortunately, there are a few eateries around the country that serve up breakfast like the regal meal it's meant to be.

MOTHER'S BISTRO & BAR Portland, Oregon

DELUCA'S Pittsburgh, Pennsylvania

THE INN ON COVENTRY Cleveland, Ohio

THE BUFF Boulder, Colorado

PANCAKE PANTRY Nashville, Tennessee

OLGA'S CUP & SAUCER Providence, Rhode Island (my sound guy and dear friend Eric also *loves* Nick's on Broadway)

THE FRIENDLY TOAST Portsmouth, New Hampshire

JIM-DENNY'S Sacramento, California

OATMEAL PANCAKES

2 cups cooked oatmeal, cooled

8 egg whites, from large eggs

2½ tablespoons pure vanilla extract

1 tablespoon ground cinnamon

¼ cup soy milk

2 cups fresh (or thawed frozen) blueberries (optional)

Serves 4 These pancakes come from a buddy I grew up with. His cousin the personal trainer gave him this easy, quick-fix breakfast recipe that not only fills you up but makes your house smell amazing. Frozen blueberries are great to have on hand; they tend to be cheaper than fresh berries, and you can have them year-round. Even served plain, the pancakes are a tasty and heart-healthy way to start the day.

1 In a small bowl, combine the oatmeal, egg whites, vanilla, cinnamon, soy milk, and blueberries, if using, stirring to create a thick, paste-like batter.

2 Lightly coat a 10-inch skillet with nonstick cooking spray and set it over medium heat. When hot, spoon in about ¼ cup of the pancake batter.

3 When the bottom is brown and firm enough to flip, approximately 3 minutes, turn the pancake with a spatula. Cook for another 2 minutes. Remove from the pan and keep warm on a plate under a clean towel. Continue making pancakes until you've used all of the batter. Serve warm.

MAPLE PECAN SYRUP

Because life is too short to have plain syrup on your pancakes. And if you use regular syrup, you can't sit with us.

¼ cup pecans

½ cup pure maple syrup

¼ teaspoon ground cinnamon

½ teaspoon vanilla extract

1. Preheat the oven to 350°F.

2. On rimmed baking sheet, spread the pecans in a single layer. Toast them until light golden brown, about 6 to 8 minutes.

3. Transfer the nuts to a bowl to cool to room temperature.

4. In a food processor, process until finely ground.

5. Add the syrup, cinnamon, and vanilla and blend until spreadable.

LEMON RICOTTA PANCAKES

Serves 4 to 6 The pancakes served at the Inn on Coventry in Cleveland, Ohio, inspired this recipe. They are at once crispy and flavorful.

2 tablespoons sugar

2 tablespoons freshly grated lemon zest

2 cups whole-milk ricotta

6 extra-large eggs, separated

½ teaspoon kosher salt

1 cup all-purpose flour, sifted

Pure maple syrup

1 In a medium bowl, combine the sugar and lemon zest. Add the ricotta, egg yolks, and salt to the bowl. Whisk until combined. Add the flour and whisk until blended.

2 In the bowl of an electric mixer fitted with the whisk attachment, beat the egg whites on medium-high speed until they form medium-firm peaks, about 3 minutes.

3 Using a rubber spatula, fold the egg whites into the ricotta mixture. Be gentle! Don't stir!

4 Lightly coat a 10-inch skillet with nonstick cooking spray and set it over medium-high heat. Pour in about ¼ cup of pancake batter.

5 When the batter has small bubbles all over the surface, after approximately 2 to 3 minutes, flip the pancake with a spatula. Cook for another 2 minutes. Remove the pancake from the pan and keep it warm on a plate under a clean towel. Continue making pancakes until you've used all of the batter.

6 Serve warm with the syrup.

ONE-PAN BREAKFAST BURRITO

4 tablespoons (½ stick) unsalted butter, divided

½ small onion, diced

1 red bell pepper, seeded and diced

1 cup canned black beans, rinsed and drained

Hot sauce to taste

Kosher salt and freshly ground black pepper to taste

8 large eggs

⅓ cup shredded pepper Jack cheese

4 large flour tortillas

¼ cup sour cream

¼ cup salsa (any kind you like)

1 large tomato, diced

1 small avocado, halved, scooped, and cubed

Serves 4 Having tried breakfast burritos from Indianapolis to Denver, I've learned that it's all about balance. It has to be a burrito—hearty, handheld, and substantial. But it's also still breakfast, so there should be fluffy, buttery lightness to the ingredients, with the right mix of richness and spice. That's what you get here.

1 In a 12-inch nonstick skillet, melt 2 tablespoons of the butter over medium-high heat. Cook the onion and pepper until the onion is translucent and the pepper is softened, about 5 minutes. Add the black beans and hot sauce and cook for another 3 minutes, stirring occasionally. Season with salt and pepper. Transfer the pan's contents to a bowl.

2 In a small bowl, whisk the eggs. Stir in the cheese. Return the skillet to medium heat, then add the remaining 2 tablespoons of butter. Once the butter has melted, reduce the heat to low and add the eggs-and-cheese mixture, whisking constantly for about 3 minutes or until the eggs are cooked to your liking.

3 Spread each tortilla with 1 spoonful each of sour cream and salsa, then layer on the black-bean mixture, scrambled eggs, diced tomato, and avocado, spreading each addition evenly. Season to taste with more hot sauce. Roll up burrito-style and serve.

HANGOVER EGG SAMMY

Serves 1 A classmate from Emory University introduced me to this dish. He first used cream stout in his eggs simply because it's what he had on hand. When I tried it myself, I realized that I could build on that flavor; the creaminess of mozzarella echoed the cream of the stout, and the tanginess of sun-dried tomatoes was a great counterpoint.

2 large eggs

½ cup cream stout, such as Sam Adams

1 tablespoon olive oil

3 sun-dried tomatoes in olive oil, drained and chopped

1 teaspoon dried oregano

Kosher salt and freshly ground black pepper to taste

¼ cup shredded fresh mozzarella

1 whole-wheat English muffin, toasted

2 slices of cooked turkey bacon (optional)

1 In a small bowl, whisk together the eggs and stout until well combined.

2 In a 12-inch skillet set over medium heat, heat the oil. Add the egg mixture, scrambling lightly. Add the sun-dried tomatoes, oregano, salt, and pepper.

3 As the eggs begin to set, add the cheese and continue to scramble to your preferred degree of doneness.

4 When the eggs are done, mound them on the bottom half of the toasted English muffin. Lay the cooked bacon slices on top of the eggs, if desired, and top with the other English muffin half. Serve hot.

BACON AND CHEDDAR FRITTATA

10 to 12 tater tots

12 large eggs, lightly beaten

1 cup shredded Cheddar cheese

⅔ cup finely diced white onions

Kosher salt and freshly ground black pepper to taste

6 slices of bacon, diced

2 tablespoons unsalted butter

⅔ cup chopped green onions, white and green parts, plus 1 or 2 tablespoons for garnish

Serves 6 I think of this as a good bachelor recipe; it shows how I often cook at home, using great things that I have on hand to make easy meals. Important note: Bake, don't fry, the tots before adding them to the egg mixture. Frying them will make your frittata unnecessarily oily and heavy.

1 Preheat the oven to 350°F.

2 Arrange the tater tots on a baking sheet and bake according to the package directions, just until crisp and browned. Let them cool, then tear them into rough chunks. Turn the oven to Broil.

3 In a medium bowl, use a fork to combine the eggs, Cheddar, white onions, salt, and pepper.

4 In a 12-inch ovenproof skillet set over medium heat, cook the bacon until crisp. Pour off the rendered fat. Add the butter to the pan and heat until melted.

5 Pour the egg mixture into the pan and stir with a wooden spoon. Cook for 3 to 4 minutes, or until the egg mixture begins to set.

6 Stir in the tater tots and green onions. Slide the pan under the broiler and cook until the eggs are lightly browned, about 3 minutes. Remove the pan from oven and cut into 6 wedges. Serve hot.

GORP-STYLE GRANOLA BARS

3½ cups rolled oats

1 cup raw unsalted peanuts

¼ cup slivered almonds

¼ cup semisweet chocolate chips

¼ cup plain M&M's

1 cup honey or light molasses

½ cup (packed) light brown sugar

½ teaspoon ground cinnamon

1 large egg, beaten

10 tablespoons unsalted butter, melted

Makes 16 bars The essence of a great granola bar is the jam used to hold it all together—I enjoy apricot the most. I don't overdo it on the fun odds and ends, because adding too many ingredients makes the bars more crumbly. These are great for an on-the-go snack.

1 Preheat the oven to 350°F.

2 Spread the oats, peanuts, and almonds on an ungreased rimmed baking sheet and bake until golden brown and toasted, 15 to 20 minutes, stirring once or twice. Leave the oven on.

3 Transfer the oats and nuts to a bowl and allow to cool for a few minutes. Add the chocolate chips, M&M's, honey, brown sugar, cinnamon, egg, and butter and mix well.

4 Generously coat a 9 × 13-inch rimmed baking sheet with nonstick cooking spray. (I sometimes use a disposable foil pan, which is easy to peel away from the finished bars should they stick to the pan.) Spread the mixture in the pan, using your fingers to press it firmly in an even layer.

5 Return the pan to the oven and bake for about 35 minutes, or until the granola is lightly browned along the edges.

6 Remove the pan from the oven and let the granola cool completely before cutting it into bars. Store the bars in an airtight container for up to 1 week.

LET'S DO LUNCH

"LET'S DO LUNCH" MAY BE A CHEESY-SOUNDING

way to invite someone break bread, but don't let that put you off lunch. It's a very special meal that we pack for our little ones or for ourselves or that we share with friends and colleagues to break up the dreary doldrums of our day. And it's a perfect opportunity to celebrate some of my all-time favorite foods: soups, sandwiches, and, of course, burgers.

I think it's a shame that for many, soup is generally consumed only when they are a bit under the weather or as the afterthought that comes with their half sandwich. Soups are actually wonderfully nuanced layers of flavor to be slurped down a spoonful at a time, and most are easier to make than you think.

Sandwiches, as I've often said, are simply your imagination bound by two pieces of bread; the only limitations are your pantry, your bread, and your appetite. Because you can score a sandwich pretty much anywhere, whether you're dining in a national chain of sandwich artists or out of a vending machine, the notion that a sandwich can be a "home-cooked meal" has largely been lost. My hope is that the fun flavors and novel approaches to sandwichery in this chapter will change that attitude.

And let's not forget the burger—the meaty masterpiece we gift to ourselves on game day and at barbecues, best consumed with buddies and brewskis and bacon. The burger has moved well beyond its humble beginnings, served on white bread and topped only with onion and tomatoes at Louis' Lunch in New Haven, Connecticut, to an artisanal work of "gastronomy." The burgers in this chapter aren't packed with pretense or pâté. They are, however, loaded with flavor and represent the endless inspiration I've derived from the delicious, meaty magnificence I have experienced in burger form both at home and abroad. Enjoy, and don't let your meat loaf.

SHRIMP SCAMPI BISQUE 27

TORTILLA SOUP with Guacamole Wontons 28

FRAWNCH ONION SOUP with Mini Roast-Beef Panini 31

BLOODY MARY GAZPACHO with Shrimp 32

CREAMY TOMATO SOUP with Grilled-Cheese Sandwich Dumplings 35

ASIAN VARIATION ON MOM'S CHICKEN SOUP
with Gribenes Crostini 37

STUFFED PITA with Lamb, Onions, and Rosemary Potatoes 40

GRILLED PITA with Fig Jam, Caramelized Onions, and Blue Cheese 41

CHILI-FRITO SLOPPY JOSÉ
with Sliced Avocado and Crunchy Pickled Onions 43

CORNMEAL FRIED OYSTER CLUB on Weck 44

THE "INFIELD" SANDWICH 47

MILWAUKEE BEER-BRAISED BRATWURST SANDWICH
with Pittsburgh-Style Slaw 48

LONDON BROIL GARLIC MAYO STEAK WRAPS 50

KENTUCKY HOT BROWN BLUEGRASS SANDWICHES 53

JUICY LUCIA 54

BÁNH MÌ BURGER 57

SPICY SLIDERS 58

GYRO BURGER with Tzatziki and Tirokafteri 60

MALBEC BURGERS with Creole Mustard Tomato Jam 62

SLOPPY 'ZO! 65

SHRIMP SCAMPI BISQUE

2 tablespoons olive oil

1 large onion, chopped

6 garlic cloves, chopped

1 bay leaf, crushed

Pinch of crushed red pepper flakes

2 quarts shrimp or shellfish stock

1½ pounds medium shrimp, peeled, deveined, and tails removed

2 cups diced day-old French bread

½ cup heavy cream

½ cup grated Parmesan cheese

Kosher salt to taste

1 tablespoon chopped fresh parsley leaves, for garnish

Serves 6 to 8 The brilliant chef Brian Landry of Borgne Restaurant in New Orleans once served me an unbelievably delicious and savory garlic-bread soup. Inspired by that and the concept of thickening sauces with old bread, and because I love dunking bread in the wonderful garlic oil that often accompanies scampi dishes, I have combined the creamy-warm deliciousness of that soup with the garlicky richness of scampi. Important note: Starting with shrimp in the shell gives the soup a much richer flavor, but do *not* forget to shell the shrimp before pureeing the bisque!

1 In a large saucepan set over medium heat, heat the olive oil. Add the onion, garlic, bay leaf, and red pepper flakes. Cook until the onion is golden, 2 to 3 minutes.

2 Stir in the stock and bring to a boil. Reduce the heat to low and simmer the soup for 30 minutes. Add the shrimp and simmer for an additional 6 minutes. Remove 6 or 8 shrimp with a slotted spoon and set them aside for garnish.

3 Turn the heat up to high. Add the bread and cream and whisk until the bread has dissolved into the soup, about 5 minutes.

4 Using a handheld blender or a food processor, puree the soup until smooth. Stir in the cheese and season with salt.

5 Ladle the soup into individual serving bowls and garnish with the reserved whole shrimp and parsley.

TORTILLA SOUP
with GUACAMOLE WONTONS

2 cups guacamole, homemade or store-bought

1 tablespoon olive oil

1 onion, chopped

3 garlic cloves, minced

1 28-ounce can of crushed tomatoes

4 cups chicken stock

8 corn tortillas, sliced into strips, divided

2 teaspoons chili powder

1 teaspoon dried oregano

¼ cup chopped fresh cilantro

1 rotisserie chicken, skin and bones discarded, meat shredded

Vegetable oil, for frying

32 round wonton wrappers

1 large egg, beaten, for egg wash

½ pound Monterey Jack or Cheddar cheese, shredded

Serves 6 to 8 I love soup dumplings and have tried them everywhere from San Francisco to Singapore. But at a restaurant in the West Village owned by Chef Anita Lo, I tried a version that involved foie gras, which taught me that if you fill your dumplings with ingredients that are either frozen or chilled, you can fry them and have the filling remain cool despite a warm, crispy exterior. I would later see this theory proven time and time again by the brilliant chefs of the California and Texas state fairs, where they fry everything from butter to soda. My guacamole dumplings are another such example and are a great addition to this soup.

1 Spread the guacamole in a shallow, freezer-safe glass dish. Cover with plastic wrap, pressing it onto the surface of the guac, and place in the freezer for at least 30 minutes, or until the guacamole is frozen almost completely solid.

2 In a medium stockpot, heat the olive oil over medium heat. Sauté the onion and garlic until soft, about 4 minutes. Stir in the tomatoes and their liquid, chicken stock, ¾ of the tortilla strips, and 1¼ cups of water. Bring the liquid to a boil. Add the chili powder, oregano, cilantro, and chicken meat. Reduce the heat to low and let simmer for 15 minutes.

3 Fill an 8-quart pot with 2 inches of vegetable oil and set it over medium heat. Using a deep-frying thermometer, heat the oil until it reaches 375°F. Line a plate or platter with paper towels and set aside.

RECIPE CONTINUES

4 Lay the wonton wrappers on a clean, dry surface. Cut the frozen guacamole into 1-tablespoon chunks. Place a guacamole cube on a wonton wrapper. Brush the edges of the wrapper with the egg wash and fold the wrapper diagonally to enclose the filling, pinching the edges to seal. Repeat with the remaining guacamole and wrappers.

5 Working in batches, if necessary, fry the guacamole wontons until the wrappers are golden and crispy, about 3 minutes per side. Place the fried wontons on the lined plate to drain.

6 Heat the remaining tortilla strips in a microwave until hot. Divide the warm strips among bowls and top with the shredded cheese. Ladle the soup into each bowl and add a few guacamole wontons to each. Serve hot.

FIRE DEPARTMENT—PUTTING OUT THE FLAMES

I know that watching me on television sweating and pounding the table, bloodshot eyes and all, is enough to scare anybody away from the spicy stuff. But that is the extreme end of the spectrum. Nobody should be eating intense spice like that regularly. However, even I have occasionally found myself ingesting something hotter than I can tolerate.

When that happens, no amount of water will wash away the volatile oils on your tongue. For removing heat from your mouth, dairy tends to work best, although it can end up wreaking havoc on your stomach. I have found that chewing a piece of bread and spitting it out has helped absorb some of the capsaicin in my gob.

And of course what goes up, must come down. There is always the fear that one may, as my grandpa used to say, "taste it twice" and feel the burn again on the way out. My best advice for avoiding this is:

- Eat bananas before consuming spicy food.

- Eat white rice directly before and after eating spicy food.

Such precautions should help you appreciate all of the exhilaration that a spicy meal can bring.

And if you are in New York City, Szechuan Gourmet on West Thirty-Ninth Street will blow your mind!

(Yunnan Garden in Las Vegas is also magnificent, as is Chengdu Taste in Alhambra, California.)

FRAWNCH ONION SOUP
with MINI ROAST-BEEF PANINI

6 slices of deli roast beef

6 slices of provolone cheese

2 large onions, sliced

12 slices of rye bread

6 to 8 tablespoons unsalted
butter, divided

Kosher salt and freshly ground
pepper to taste

2 tablespoons all-purpose
flour

8 cups beef broth

1 cup dry white wine

12 slices of Swiss cheese

Serves 6 I'm fairly well versed in the ways of onion soup, and one of the best I've had was at Bern's Steak House in Tampa, Florida. Now, personally, I happen to love dunking sandwiches in soup, but grilling a panini (which seals the sandwich from the brunt of the sogginess factor) and putting it at the bottom of the bowl provides a great surprise.

1 Make 6 sandwiches: For each, layer a slice of roast beef, provolone, and onion between two slices of rye bread.

2 In a large skillet, melt a tablespoon of butter over medium-high heat. Working in batches with more butter as needed, grill the sandwiches, pressing down on them with a spatula like a panini until golden brown on both sides, about 7 minutes. Refrigerate until cool.

3 In a large pot set over medium heat, melt 3 tablespoons of the butter. Add the remaining onion slices and a large pinch of salt, and cook, stirring occasionally, until the onions are slightly caramelized and soft, 4 to 5 minutes.

4 Set the oven to Broil. Add the flour to the onions and stir to coat. Add the broth and the wine and bring to a boil. Reduce the heat to a simmer and let the onions cook until soft, for 15 minutes or so. Season with salt and pepper.

5 Place one sandwich in the bottom of each of 6 oven-safe crocks or onion soup bowls. Ladle the soup over the sandwiches. Top each serving with two slices of Swiss cheese; the cheese should fully cover the surface. Place the bowls on a rimmed baking sheet lined with foil and broil until the cheese begins to bubble and melt, about 3 minutes. Serve hot.

BLOODY MARY GAZPACHO
with SHRIMP

6 ripe plum tomatoes, chopped

1 red onion, diced

1 cucumber, peeled, seeded, and chopped

1 red bell pepper, seeded and chopped

2 celery stalks, diced

1 garlic clove, minced

¼ cup olive oil

¼ cup olive juice (from a jar of green olives)

1 tablespoon Tabasco sauce

2 tablespoons freshly squeezed lemon juice

½ cup chopped fresh cilantro leaves

Kosher salt and freshly ground black pepper to taste

1 pound small shrimp, peeled

½ cup vodka

½ cup Worcestershire sauce

2 tablespoons unsalted butter

Serves 6 I have always appreciated the refreshing nature of cold gazpacho—and the novel notion that a soup could serve as a refreshment (one of the reasons I love and appreciate Korean iced naengmyeon noodles)—and with a splash of vodka stirred in, it evokes the bite of a classic Bloody Mary. The warm shrimp add texture, and I love the hot-cold combo. You need the juice from a jar of green olives for the soup; a couple of the olives on a toothpick, or any classic Bloody Mary garnish, would work with this dish, too.

1 In a large bowl, combine the tomatoes, onion, cucumber, bell pepper, celery, garlic, olive oil, olive juice, Tabasco, lemon juice, and cilantro. Season with salt and pepper.

2 Using a hand blender, blend the ingredients until well combined in a soup-like consistency. Place the mixture in a nonmetallic, nonreactive container, cover tightly, and refrigerate for at least 4 hours or overnight to let the flavors blend.

3 About an hour before serving, in a shallow bowl combine the shrimp, vodka, and Worcestershire sauce. Cover the bowl and refrigerate for 30 minutes.

4 Strain the shrimp from the marinade and pat it dry. Discard the marinade.

5 In a large skillet set over high heat, melt the butter. Add the shrimp to the skillet and sauté until fully cooked, 3 to 4 minutes.

6 Ladle the gazpacho into individual serving bowls. Divide the hot shrimp among the bowls and stir to combine. Serve immediately.

CREAMY TOMATO SOUP
with GRILLED-CHEESE SANDWICH DUMPLINGS

10 plum tomatoes, halved lengthwise, seeds removed

4 tablespoons olive oil, divided

1 onion, diced

4 garlic cloves, chopped

2 28-ounce cans of crushed San Marzano tomatoes

3 cups vegetable stock

1½ cups heavy cream

Kosher salt and freshly ground black pepper to taste

6 slices of American cheese

12 slices of Wonder Bread

2 to 4 tablespoons unsalted butter

Serves 6 I came across *The Wonder Bread Cookbook* while filming in Omaha, Nebraska, and, among its many amazing qualities, I learned that you could make a pocket or ravioli with this super soft and squishy bread simply by crimping the edge with a fork. Since the white bread grilled-cheese sandwich is among the best things ever, and undoubtedly the very best accompaniment to tomato soup, I was inspired to make mini grilled-cheese sandwiches to float in this soup like dumplings. It creates the "hey, that's pretty darn cool!" visual element and delivers a new take on a classic comfort food combo.

1 Preheat the oven to 325°F.

2 Place the plum tomatoes in a large baking dish. Drizzle with 2 tablespoons of the olive oil. Roast until the tomatoes are soft, 25 to 30 minutes.

3 In a large stockpot set over medium heat, heat the remaining 2 tablespoons of olive oil. Add the onion and garlic and cook until the onion is soft, about 5 minutes.

4 Add the roasted tomatoes and their juices, the canned tomatoes and their juices, and the stock, and bring to a boil. Reduce the heat to a simmer, stir in the cream, and season with salt and pepper. Simmer the soup for 10 minutes.

5 Remove the pot from the heat and use a handheld blender to puree the soup until it's as smooth or as chunky as you prefer. (If you don't have a handheld blender, you can use a potato masher to break up the tomatoes, or you can crush them against the side of the pot with a wooden spoon.)

RECIPE CONTINUES

CREAMY TOMATO SOUP
CONTINUED

6   Make 6 sandwiches with 1 slice of cheese between slices
    of the white bread. Cut off the crusts and cut each sandwich
    into quarters. Crimp the edges of the bread together with
    a fork to make little packets that enclose the cheese. You
    should have 24 cheese dumplings.

7   In a large skillet set over medium-high heat, melt a
    tablespoon of the butter. Working in batches and adding more
    butter as needed, grill the cheese dumplings until they are
    browned and toasted like little grilled-cheese sandwiches.

8   Ladle the soup into 6 bowls and top with the dumplings.
    Serve immediately.

ASIAN VARIATION ON MOM'S CHICKEN SOUP
with GRIBENES CROSTINI

Serves 4 to 6 Like most Jewish boys, I love my mother's chicken soup, and I'm also a big fan of bright Asian flavors like green onion, ginger, and Sriracha, all great complements to traditional chicken soup. This version combines flavors from my youth with those of the Asian soups I have come to know and love as an adult.

FOR THE SOUP

1 tablespoon vegetable oil

1 whole chicken (about 4 pounds), quartered

1 large onion, roughly chopped

4 celery stalks, roughly chopped

4 carrots, roughly chopped

1 turnip, peeled and chopped

5 garlic cloves, roughly chopped

1 bunch of fresh flat-leaf parsley

1 bunch of fresh dill

2 tablespoons miso paste

Kosher salt and white pepper to taste

FOR THE GRIBENES CROSTINI

1 large onion, chopped

Reserved chicken breast skin

Kosher salt to taste

4 slices of challah, toasted

TO SERVE

4 to 6 ounces cellophane noodles, soaked in cool water for 20 minutes

Breast meat from a rotisserie chicken, shredded

2 green onions, white and green parts, minced

Sriracha to taste

1 Make the soup: In a large pot set over medium-high heat, heat the oil. Once the oil is shimmering, add the chicken legs and thighs from the quartered chicken and a fourth of the chopped onions. Cook without moving for 1 or 2 minutes, then stir and continue to cook until the chicken pieces are browned all over. Remove the chicken from the pot. Add the celery, carrots, and the remainder of the onions. Reduce the heat to low, cover, and cook until the carrots are soft, about 3 minutes. Uncover, add the turnip and garlic, and cook for a few minutes until all the veggies are soft.

RECIPE CONTINUES

Hong Kong

Phuket THAILAND

2 Return the browned chicken pieces to the pot along with the breast and wing quarters. Fill the pot with water to cover the chicken. Add the parsley and dill. Bring to a low boil over high heat, then reduce the heat and simmer uncovered for 1 hour.

3 Make the gribenes: In a heavy skillet set over low heat, place the chopped onion and the reserved skin from the chicken breast and cook for 20 to 30 minutes, stirring occasionally, until the fat is rendered. Turn the heat to medium-high and continue to cook until the onions and skin are golden brown, about 3 minutes. Sprinkle with kosher salt. Using a slotted spoon, remove the crispy skin and onions from the pan and place them on heavy paper to drain. Once cool, finely mince the skin and onions.

4 Strain the soup, discarding the solids, and return the broth to the pot. Bring back to a boil, skim off any fat that rises to the surface, and lower the heat to a simmer. Whisk in the miso paste and taste. If necessary, add salt and pepper. Keep warm.

5 To serve: Divide the cellophane noodles among individual bowls and ladle the hot soup on top. Sprinkle with the chicken and chopped green onions, and add Sriracha to taste. Spread the toasted challah with gribenes and serve alongside the soup.

STUFFED PITA
with LAMB, ONIONS, and ROSEMARY POTATOES

4 Yukon Gold potatoes, peeled and halved

½ cup olive oil

¼ cup fresh rosemary leaves

5 tablespoons vegetable oil, divided

2 tablespoons ground cumin

1½ teaspoons crushed red pepper flakes

1 tablespoon soy sauce

1 tablespoon cornstarch

2 teaspoons toasted sesame oil

1 teaspoon sugar

Kosher salt and freshly ground black pepper to taste

1¼ pounds ground lamb

1 large white onion, cut into 1½-inch pieces

4 pita bread pockets

Serves 4 Like nearly everyone in the food space, I have an abiding love for the gristly, bristly, sardonic, peripatetic, ascerbic sage that is Anthony Bourdain. Long ago, before I had embarked on my food journeys and challenges, I saw a show in which Tony dined on the sands of the African desert with a Berber tribe, eating a stuffed, spiced, layered loaf of ground-lamb-filled bread that had been baked in an earthen oven. I became obsessed with what those flavors might be and how I could play with them and try my own variant. This pita may not channel Tony with nomadic tribes on oceans of sand, but it is really, really delicious.

1 Place the potatoes in a large saucepan with water to cover. Bring to a boil, then reduce the heat to a simmer and cook until the potatoes can be easily pierced with a fork, 12 to 15 minutes. Drain the potatoes in a colander.

2 In the same saucepan, heat the olive oil over medium heat. Add the rosemary, and when it becomes fragrant, after about 1 minute, return the potatoes to the pan. Mash the potatoes with a masher or fork. Season to taste and keep warm.

3 In a large bowl, combine 4 tablespoons of the vegetable oil with the cumin, red pepper flakes, soy sauce, cornstarch, sesame oil, sugar, and a pinch of salt and pepper. Add the lamb and onions and combine thoroughly. Let stand for 10 minutes.

4 Heat a large cast-iron pan over high heat. Add the remaining tablespoon of vegetable oil and tilt the pan to cover the bottom with oil. Add the seasoned lamb and onions and cook, breaking the meat up with a wooden spoon, until browned, 8 to 10 minutes. You will have a mixture like seasoned taco filling.

5 Toast the pitas. Slice them open on one end and stuff with the potatoes and then the lamb and onions. Slice into wedges like a pizza pie and serve hot.

GRILLED PITA with FIG JAM, CARAMELIZED ONIONS, AND BLUE CHEESE

2 tablespoons olive oil, plus more for brushing the pitas

1 large onion, sliced

4 pocketless pitas

½ cup fig jam (recipe below)

1 cup creamy blue cheese, such as Saga

1 bunch of watercress, washed, dried, and chilled

Serves 2 to 4 One of the first kitchens I ever worked in had a sandwich that featured fig jam and brie. Since then, I have been obsessed with using fig jam as a condiment—not just because of how well it pairs with cheese, but because its seeds mirror the crunchiness of whole-grain mustard. With just six ingredients, this recipe has a hint of the party cheese plate about it; it can function as an entrée by itself, served with a salad and a glass of white wine, or you can slice it like a pizza and serve it as an appetizer.

1 Preheat the oven to 400°F.

2 In a large skillet, heat the oil. Add the onion and cook over low to medium-low heat until golden, but not blackened, 8 to 12 minutes. Remove the skillet from the heat.

3 Place the pitas on a baking sheet and brush them with olive oil. Toast in the oven for about 3 minutes, or until slightly crisp.

4 Remove the pitas from the oven and spread fig jam over each. Top with the caramelized onions and blue cheese. Return the pitas to the oven until fully toasted, about 3 minutes.

5 Top with the cold watercress. Cut each pita into quarters and serve immediately.

FRESH FIG JAM

1 pound fresh figs

¾ cup sugar

¼ cup water

3 tablespoons fresh lemon juice

1 Trim the stems from the figs and chop into small pieces.

2 In a small saucepan, toss the chopped figs with the sugar. Let the mixture stand for 10 minutes, then add the water and lemon juice.

3 Bring the mixture to a boil over medium heat and cook for about 20 minutes, stirring now and then, until the figs are soft and the liquid has thickened.

4 Cool and transfer the jam to a covered container. Refrigerate in an airtight container for up to 2 weeks.

CHILI-FRITO SLOPPY JOSÉ
with SLICED AVOCADO and CRUNCHY PICKLED ONIONS

¼ cup olive oil

2 pounds ground beef

1 medium yellow onion, chopped

4 garlic cloves, crushed

2 tablespoons ground cumin

2 tablespoons chili powder

1 teaspoon cayenne pepper

Kosher salt and freshly ground black pepper to taste

1 16-ounce can of whole tomatoes

1 large bag of Fritos corn chips

1 pound Cheddar cheese, shredded

6 potato rolls

1 avocado, peeled, pitted, and sliced

Pickled Red Onions (page 179) to taste

Serves 6 I first encountered the delicacy known as chili Frito pie while working with the Texas State Fair. It is essentially a much thicker sloppy joe with southwestern seasonings, a backbone of velvety cheese, and a layer of everyone's favorite corn chip in a somewhat soggy, somewhat crunchy, entirely salty incarnation. To balance the richness of the chili Frito pie itself, as well as the butteriness of the avocado I love to add to any southwestern dish I serve, I've thrown in a classic Mexican taqueria condiment: pickled red onions. I highly recommend making a large batch of these, because not only will they keep for several weeks, but they also make an unusually great addition to any meal—even Chinese takeout! You can make the chili ahead of time and then assemble and bake the casserole right before serving.

1 In a large pot set over high heat, heat the oil. Add the ground beef and onion and sauté until the meat is browned, 4 to 5 minutes.

2 Add the garlic, cumin, chili powder, cayenne, salt, and pepper, and stir to combine. Cook for 2 more minutes, stirring occasionally. Add the canned tomatoes and their juices and bring to a boil. Reduce the heat to a simmer and cook for 30 minutes, breaking up the tomatoes with a spoon.

3 Preheat the oven to 350°F.

4 Spread the corn chips evenly on the bottom of a rectangular baking dish. Pour the chili over the chips, top with the shredded cheese, and bake until the cheese is fully melted, 4 to 6 minutes.

5 To serve: Scoop the Frito chili onto potato rolls and serve the sandwiches topped with sliced avocado and pickled red onion.

CORNMEAL FRIED OYSTER CLUB ON WECK

Makes 2 sandwiches While many states in the South do justice to the fried oyster, my favorite is found in the heart of the Big Easy, New Orleans. Perhaps no finer oyster can be found than the one at Stanley Restaurant in Jackson Square, though I must acknowledge the excellent job done by Parkway Bakery, Domilise's, and Short Stop Poboys in Metairie. They maintain the briny unctuousness of the oyster and add a crunchy exterior of cornmeal and the awesome texture that comes with it, without going too far in either direction. Playing off the universal appeal of the club sandwich, I add the traditional bacon, lettuce, tomato, and avocado accoutrements to my oyster sandwich and serve it on Buffalo's signature roll, the weck (see page 51). Combined with the fried oysters, this is one truly epic sandwich.

1 cup masa

1 cup buttermilk

1 cup cornmeal

1 dozen oysters, shucked

2 kaiser rolls

1 egg white, from large egg, beaten

2 tablespoons kosher salt

2 tablespoons caraway seeds

Peanut oil, for frying

2 tablespoons mayonnaise

4 romaine lettuce leaves

1 tomato, sliced

4 slices of bacon, cooked until crisp

1 ripe avocado, halved, pitted, and sliced

1 Preheat the oven to 350°F.

2 Place the masa, buttermilk, and cornmeal in three separate bowls. Dip the oysters first in the masa, then in the buttermilk, and then finally in the cornmeal, coating completely. Let them sit for 5 minutes.

3 Brush the tops of the rolls with the egg white and set on an ungreased baking sheet. Top the rolls with the salt and caraway seeds. Toast in the oven for about 2 minutes.

4 Fill a deep saucepan with about 3 inches of peanut oil and heat to 350°F (use a deep fryer or a candy thermometer to check the temperature).

5 Fry the oysters in the hot oil, working in batches if necessary, until golden brown, about 3 minutes per batch. Remove the oysters to a paper towel–lined plate.

6 Slice the rolls open and spread the tops and bottoms with mayonnaise. Pile on the lettuce, tomato slices, bacon, oysters, and avocado slices. Serve warm.

THE "INFIELD" SANDWICH

4 cups shredded roast pork
(see Myron Mixon Pork
Shoulder the Easy Way,
page 126, for a superb
recipe)

1 cup barbecue sauce

1 cup maple syrup

8 store-bought waffles

4 slices of Cheddar cheese

Serves 4 This was actually a last-minute creation during an episode of *Man v. Food* we shot for the Daytona 500—hence the nickname. At Slows Bar B Q in Detroit, I noticed how the chef would pull chicken for his sandwiches off the bone and toss it with sauce in a skillet; that way, the sauce covers each bit of meat and has a chance to caramelize in the pan. I had the sudden stroke of sandwich inspiration to use the same technique with smoky pulled pork and put it all together with maple syrup, sharp Cheddar, and the crunchy, pillowy goodness of a breakfast waffle. Who could resist?

1 Preheat the oven to 325°F.

2 Put the shredded meat in a baking pan. Toss with the barbecue sauce and maple syrup, reserving a few tablespoons of each. Place the pan in the oven to heat through.

3 Toast the waffles until crisp. Arrange half the waffles on a baking sheet, top each with a slice of cheese, and slide into the oven. Bake until the cheese melts, about 5 minutes.

4 Top each cheesy waffle with some of the pulled pork and a drizzle of the reserved barbecue sauce and maple syrup. Top with another waffle and serve hot.

MILWAUKEE BEER-BRAISED BRATWURST SANDWICH
with PITTSBURGH-STYLE SLAW

Serves 4 In Green Bay's Lambeau Field stadium, there is a restaurant called Curly's Pub, named for the great Packers coach Curly Lambeau. Tailgating culture is extremely strong in the great state of Wisconsin, and the sovereign meat product of a Wisconsin tailgate is the bratwurst. At Curly's Pub I saw the brats braised slowly with beer and onions, which added a depth of sweetness and flavor. The slaw is inspired by the great Primanti Bros. restaurant in Pittsburgh. Slaw appears on all their sandwiches (along with French fries, of course). It's got a wonderful bracing acidity and is more of an Italian salad than your traditional mayonnaise-based picnic slaw.

FOR THE SLAW

1 pound green cabbage, shredded

¼ cup sugar

½ tablespoon kosher salt

¼ teaspoon celery seed

¼ cup vegetable oil

¼ cup apple cider vinegar

Freshly ground black pepper to taste

FOR THE BRATS

4 bratwurst links

1 onion, sliced

2 12-ounce bottles of beer

4 hoagie rolls, toasted

Spicy mustard to taste (optional)

1 Combine the cabbage, sugar, salt, and celery seed in a colander set over a bowl. Let stand for at least 1 hour and up to 4 hours to let the cabbage fully wilt and release its juices.

2 Transfer the wilted cabbage to a clean bowl (discard any remaining liquid). Add the oil and vinegar and toss to coat. Season with pepper to taste.

3 Put the brats and the onion in a large Dutch oven and cover with the beer. Place over high heat and bring to a boil. Reduce the heat to a simmer and cook until the brats are fully cooked, about 20 minutes.

4 Stuff the toasted rolls with the brats and onions. Top with the cabbage slaw and some spicy mustard, if using, and serve.

LONDON BROIL GARLIC MAYO STEAK WRAPS

FOR THE STEAK MARINADE

½ cup brewed black coffee, cooled to room temperature

1 tablespoon balsamic vinegar

½ cup dry red wine

⅓ cup soy sauce

4 garlic cloves, crushed

FOR THE LONDON BROIL

2 pounds London broil

1 head of green cabbage, leaves separated, rinsed, and spun dry

Roasted Garlic Mayo (page 186)

1 can of sliced water chestnuts, drained

Serves 6 I came up with this recipe as a young actor looking to stretch out groceries, keep carbs low, and buy ingredients that would yield several meals. London broil is not a very expensive cut of meat (any time you see the word *round*, it means leaner meat), and cabbage is downright inexpensive and very good for you. The cabbage leaf wrap with the creamy garlic mayo is a very refreshing complement to this tasty London broil. These wraps are a very crispy snack not unlike a Vietnamese spring roll. They are great hot or cold.

1 Make the marinade: In a large, sealable plastic bag, combine the coffee, vinegar, red wine, soy sauce, and crushed garlic cloves. Seal and shake to combine.

2 Make the London broil: Poke the steak with a knife in a few places to help it absorb the marinade. Put the meat in the bag, seal, and refrigerate for at least 4 hours and up to 24 hours.

3 Preheat the oven to 350°F. Remove the steak from the marinade and allow it to come to room temperature, reserving the marinade separately.

4 Heat a cast-iron skillet over high heat and when hot, add the steak. Sear for 3 to 4 minutes on one side. Turn and sear the second side for another 3 to 4 minutes. Baste the meat with the marinade and place the skillet in the oven for 7 minutes for a rare steak, 12 minutes for medium well. Remove the skillet from the oven and let the steak rest in the pan for 10 minutes, then slice the meat thinly. Discard any remaining marinade.

5 To make each wrap, place a slice or two of steak in the center of a cabbage leaf. Add a dollop of garlic mayo and a few slices of water chestnut. Roll like a burrito and serve.

REGIONAL BEEF SANDWICHES

We all know that Buffalo is where we should head to sample the smoky, spicy wing that started it all, just as we know that Baltimore is still the last word on crab cakes and Chicago is where the best deep-dish pizza and Chicago-style hot dogs can be found. But did you know that each of these places boasts a regional beef sandwich that is every bit as beloved by the locals as these other iconic foods? True. Let's meet a few other local heroes.

Baltimore is known for **pit beef**—a charcoal pit–roasted battleship round of beef, charred to a crisp blackish-brown on the outside and a buttery, ridiculously juicy pink on the inside. The meat is sliced thin and is usually served on a soft roll with crunchy slivers of raw white onion, with the key addition of "war sauce." Essentially horseradish mayo, the success of any given batch of war sauce hinges on the consistency (how thick or thin it is). It's a skill learned through year after year of doing, and the outcome differs from family to family. My favorite is Chaps Pit Beef, located on Baltimore's Pit Beef Alley—a stretch of Pulaski Highway, it must be said, in the shadow of a large, um, exotic dance establishment.

Buffalo, New York, is home to the world famous Anchor Bar, birthplace of the buffalo wing. Legend has it that dish came to be when the owner's friends came into the bar late one night and he asked his mom to make them something to eat. Since the wings were frozen, Mom deep-fried them and sauced them with some cayenne-vinegar-salt hot sauce mixed with margarine. And while this relatively simple feat of cooking has reached worldwide renown, to locals there is another delicious *revered* foodstuff that is seldom encountered outside that part of Western New York State: that would be **beef on weck**.

What the heck is weck, you ask?

A fair question. It's short for *Kümmelweck*, *Kümmel* being German for caraway, and *Weck* being the southern German word for a type of roll similar to our kaiser roll. The coarse salt and caraway seed–coated roll is topped with thin slices of rare, slow-roasted beef, and the top half of the bun is usually dipped in the rich jus from the roast. The recipe is said to hail from a bar on the Buffalo waterfront, where the German proprietor opted to serve his beef sandwich atop a salty kümmelweck in order to sell more drinks. He got more money, and mankind got this sandwich—win, win.

Buffalo's beef is a bit of a secret. Schwabl's is the name most often heard in relation to this sandwich, restaurant-wise, and the Buffalo natives with whom I am close friends have also sung the praises of the awesomely named Charlie the Butcher's Kitchen. Wherever you try it, beef on weck is always served up with a bit of hot horseradish, which I've been told is *only* to be spread on the *top* half of the roll, and is accompanied by a kosher pickle spear.

Which brings us to Chicago. Yes, they have deep dish. Yes, they put a whole pickle on a hot dog. Yes, both are worth trying with gusto, I might add. But the **Italian beef** sandwich must not be overlooked. Marinated roast beef, sliced razor thin and nearly falling apart in a silky, spicy, broth-like gravy, is piled on a chewy, seedless Italian roll that has itself been dunked in the aforementioned sexy-ass gravy. Spicy, vinegary, chunky giardiniera and sweet peppers complete the picture. It's a sandwich as much inhaled as eaten, as much drunk as it is chewed, a glorious juicy, dripping loaf of all that is good in the world, or at least that part of the Midwest. I like Al's Beef. Doug Psaltis, a badass chef in Chicago, loves Mr. Beef on Orleans. To be honest, I haven't compared the two, but I have a feeling, much as with love, that nothing compares to your first.

KENTUCKY HOT BROWN BLUEGRASS SANDWICHES

Looavul.
Luhvul.
Loueville.
Looaville.
Looeyville.
Louisville

3 tablespoons unsalted butter, plus 1 tablespoon softened for basting

⅓ cup bourbon

1 half turkey breast, about 3 pounds

Kosher salt

12 to 16 slices of Texas toast

4 plum tomatoes, sliced

Candied Bourbon Bacon (see page 180)

Mornay Sauce (see page 184)

Makes 6 to 8 sandwiches I have spent some time living in the great city of Louisville, Kentucky, where I became well acquainted with the iconic Louisville Hot Brown, created at the Brown Hotel as late-night comfort food for the revelers dancing at the Brown's ballroom. Traditionally, it is served open-faced with the turkey, béchamel or Mornay sauce, thick-cut bacon, and sliced tomato served over Texas toast. I've made it a handheld treat and glazed the turkey with bourbon-honey butter.

1 In a large pot over medium heat, melt 3 tablespoons of butter. Once it begins to foam, remove it from the heat and pour in the bourbon. Whisk to combine and let cool.

2 Preheat the oven to 400°F.

3 Using a kitchen injector, inject about 2 tablespoons of the bourbon butter into the turkey breast. Place the breast on a rimmed baking sheet and season with salt.

4 Place the baking sheet in the oven, and roast the breast for 15 minutes, then take the sheet out of the oven and rub the breast with the remaining 1 tablespoon of the bourbon butter. Place the sheet back in the oven and let the breast roast for another 30 minutes, basting three or four times with bourbon butter, until the outside is golden brown and the juices run clear when the breast is pierced. Remove from the oven and let rest.

5 When the breast is cool, cut it into thin slices. Keep the slices ready to reheat for serving.

6 To serve, place a few slices of warm turkey on a slice of bread. Top with tomato slices and a few pieces of candied bacon.

7 Either spoon some of the hot Mornay sauce over each sandwich or serve with a small pitcher of the heated sauce so your guests can dress it themselves. Top with another slice of toast and serve.

JUICY LUCIA

Serves 6 The Juicy Lucy is easily the Twin Cities' most iconic burger. This cheese-filled masterpiece has been the subject of feverish debate for generations, with two iconic spots claiming to be its originator: Matt's Bar and the 5-8 Club. To avoid any potential partisan affiliation, I offer up a variation that bears no resemblance to either of those progenitors but pays tribute nonetheless. This Italian version combines bulk Italian sausage with ground beef as well as fresh basil and roasted peppers, and it's stuffed with fresh mozzarella cheese.

1 pound ground beef

¾ teaspoon salt

½ teaspoon freshly ground black pepper

2 garlic cloves, minced

1 teaspoon liquid smoke

1 pound hot Italian pork sausage, casings removed

½ pound fresh mozzarella cheese

1 cup fresh basil, cut into thin chiffonade slices

3 roasted red peppers (see page 107)

6 semolina rolls

Olive oil, for grilling the rolls

Roasted Garlic Mayo (page 186)

1 Mix the beef with the salt, pepper, garlic, liquid smoke, and sausage meat. Form into 12 thin patties, each roughly 5 inches in diameter.

2 Cut the cheese into 6 slices and place 1 slice on top of half the patties. Top the cheese with some basil, half a roasted red pepper, and finish with a second meat patty. Crimp the edges of the patties to enclose the stuffing, making sure no cheese is exposed.

3 Chill the patties for about 15 minutes. Preheat your grill or a cast-iron skillet to medium high.

4 Place the patties on the grill and cook until medium and no longer red in the center, about 6 minutes on each side. While the burgers are cooking, brush the cut sides of each roll with olive oil and grill or toast until golden.

5 To serve, place the burgers in the grilled rolls and top with a dollop of the garlic mayo.

BÁNH MÌ BURGER

½ pound ground pork

1 tablespoon Asian five-spice powder

Kosher salt and freshly ground black pepper to taste

1 tablespoon olive oil

2 small baguettes, split lengthwise and toasted

4 slices of Canadian bacon

10 ounces pork pâté, halved lengthwise

½ cup shredded carrots

½ cup shredded pickled daikon

½ cup fresh cilantro leaves

4 romaine lettuce leaves

1 cup Hellmann's Light Mayonnaise

1 tablespoon Sriracha

Serves 2 The bánh mì has got to be one of my all-time favorite sandwiches. This burger-ized version contains juicy pork, pickled vegetables, and pâté, evoking the flavors of this Vietnamese classic in an all-American package.

1 In a large bowl, season the ground pork with the five-spice powder, salt, and pepper. Shape the seasoned meat into 2 patties.

2 Heat a cast-iron skillet over high heat. Add the olive oil and tilt the pan to cover the bottom. Sear the patties on both sides until cooked throughout, 5 to 7 minutes. Halve the burgers crosswise and arrange 2 halves on each split baguette.

3 In the same skillet, heat the Canadian bacon until hot and crispy. Layer the bacon on top of the burger halves, followed by pâté, carrots, daikon, cilantro, and lettuce.

4 Stir together the mayonnaise and Sriracha and spread over the top baguette half. Place atop the sandwich and serve hot.

BURGERLICIOUS

At its most fundamental a burger is nothing more than ground beef formed into a patty, cooked, and served on a bun. But that's only the baseline for greatness. The following places elevate that simple formula to an art form, sometimes with extravagant toppings, other times simply by virtue of the purity of their approach. Here are a few of my favorite spots throughout the country, and one outside it!

LOUIS' LUNCH New Haven, Connecticut (first hamburger ever!)

YEAH! BURGER Atlanta, Georgia

FATHER'S OFFICE Santa Monica, California

LE TUB Hollywood, Florida

THE BURGER JOINT New York City, New York

TED'S RESTAURANT Meriden, Connecticut

RED MILL BURGERS Seattle, Washington

GABBY'S BURGERS & FRIES Nashville, Tennessee

CASINO EL CAMINO Austin, Texas

THE ROCKS RESTAURANT, GOLDEN ROCK INN Nevis, West Indies

BRENNAN & CARR Brooklyn, New York

IN-N-OUT BURGER various locations throughout the western United States

5 NAPKIN BURGER New York City, New York

SPICY SLIDERS

2 or 3 habanero chiles or to taste

2 or 3 jalapeños or to taste

1 tablespoon olive oil

½ pound ground pork

½ pound ground beef

½ teaspoon salt

¼ teaspoon freshly ground black pepper

½ teaspoon cayenne powder

1 tablespoon chili powder

1 tablespoon ground cumin

½ cup Sriracha

1 cup ketchup

10 small brioche rolls

10 slices of pepper Jack cheese

Makes 10 sliders Ever since college I have appreciated the value of the handheld four-bite, late-night, drunk-food masterpiece that is the slider. I created these for a talk show appearance, and I wanted to merge the slider's handy format with the flavors of spicy Italian sausage and mozzarella, which I love. The spice balances the greasy richness inherent in a slider pretty darn well. I use more chiles, but you can adjust to your own preferences.

1 Preheat your grill (if you are cooking inside, use a cast-iron skillet or grill pan).

2 Cut in half and remove the stems from the habanero and jalapeño peppers. Place a large piece of aluminum foil on your work surface, put the cut peppers in the center, and drizzle with the olive oil. Bring the sides together and fold several times, then fold the open ends to form a package.

3 Grill the package until the peppers are thoroughly roasted, about 25 minutes. (If cooking inside, place the packet on a foil-lined baking sheet and roast the peppers in a preheated 350°F oven for 40 minutes.)

4 Remove the peppers and let cool. Discard the stems—and some of the seeds if you want to moderate the heat—then chop finely. Set aside.

5 Combine the ground pork and beef and season with the salt and black pepper. Add the chopped roasted peppers and mix well. Using your hands, make 10 small patties.

6 In a separate small bowl, combine the cayenne, chili powder, and cumin. Gently roll each patty in the spices.

7 In another small bowl, combine the Sriracha and ketchup. Mix well and set aside.

8 Place the patties on a hot grill. Baste the tops with the Sriracha-ketchup sauce. After 2 to 3 minutes, flip the burgers

and baste again with the sauce. Repeat until cooked to your desired doneness, about 5 minutes for medium-rare. (Don't be misled by the dark exteriors of the burgers, as the coating will blacken before the interior is cooked through.)

9 When the burgers are nearly finished, toast the buns on the grill. Place a slice of cheese on each burger and cook until it is melted. Assemble the sliders, placing a dollop of the remaining Sriracha-ketchup mixture on top of each burger.

EATING SPICY FOOD

A lot of people don't like spicy food. I understand that. I don't judge. Some people feel it masks the flavor of what they're eating. Of course, some people are just great big wusses.

I'm sorry . . . I had to say it.

Spicy food is something you acquire a taste for. After all, none of us was weaned on spicy food. It's something you build up a bit of a tolerance for, just as the Dread Pirate Roberts developed a resistance to iocane powder in *The Princess Bride*. And it's a bit of a rush when your food bites back a little—literally; spicy foods actually stimulate circulation and raise body temperature.

I know I have gained a reputation as the man with the asbestos mouth, but it's not just about culinary exhilaration. Capsaicin, the element that gives spicy foods their heat, has actually been linked with such health benefits as:

- **raising metabolism**

- **fighting the negative effects of LDL (bad) cholesterol and inflammation**

- **killing cancerous or leukemic cells**

- **increasing blood flow throughout the body**

- **easing depression and stress through increased secretion of serotonin (that feel-good juice our bodies produce!)**

If you're not a fan (yet), here is my advice: Find a hot sauce that is not all flame but has actual flavor, like Tabasco, Sriracha, or Frank's Red Hot. First, try it with a fatty or rich food—something like brisket or pulled pork is perfect in this capacity, though my buddy John prefers crackers with cream cheese as a canvas for testing hot sauce. Then try just a drop and see if you can find the flavor behind the flame. Many of the peppers we have been taught to fear have an incredible complexity. Habanero peppers have a wonderful citrus element, and many dried chiles from Mexico have a delicious nuttiness, woodiness, or flavor reminiscent of a rich tomato sauce.

Each time you taste the hot sauce, try a little bit more. Before you know it, you will crave hot sauce on damn near everything!

GYRO BURGER
with TZATZIKI and TIROKAFTERI

2 pounds ground lamb

⅓ cup stemmed, minced fresh oregano

1 cup stemmed, chopped fresh dill

2 teaspoons sea salt

¼ pound feta cheese, crumbled

8 pocketless pita breads

Olive oil

3 plum tomatoes, seeded and sliced

½ head of iceberg lettuce, shredded

1 cup Tzatziki or Tirokafteri (recipes follow)

Hot sauce to taste

Serves 8 In Brooklyn, where I live, there is no shortage of great Greek food—most of the city's diners are owned by Greek families who introduced me to the delicious wonders of grilled lamb with spices at a very early age. Pairing traditional Greek ingredients like feta and lamb creates a very cohesive flavor, with temperature and textural contrasts that add up to a one-of-a-kind burger experience. To top the burgers you have your choice of condiments: the cool yogurt and cucumber garlickyness of tzatziki sauce is familiar to many, but less well known is the creamy spicy feta spread known as tirokafteri, easily one of the most underrated condiments out there.

1 In a large bowl, combine the ground lamb, oregano, half of the dill, salt, and the crumbled feta. Shape the mixture into 8 flat oval patties.

2 Heat your grill or cast-iron skillet. Put the patties on the grill and cook, uncovered, for 5 minutes. Flip when necessary and cook for another 5 minutes—do *not* press on the patties as they cook, or you'll lose all the juices.

3 Brush the pitas with olive oil and throw them on the grill or in a toaster oven to lightly toast.

4 To build the burgers, place a lamb patty on the center of each pita. Cover with sliced tomatoes, shredded lettuce, the reserved dill, and a couple of dollops of tzatziki or tirokafteri. Add hot sauce, if so desired.

TIROKAFTERI

Makes approximately 1 cup

This also works as a dip, a sandwich spread, or a topping for grilled lamb.

8 ounces feta cheese
1 tablespoon plain Greek yogurt
1 tablespoon extra-virgin olive oil
1 tablespoon red wine vinegar
1 garlic clove, minced
½ teaspoon dried oregano
1 to 2 tablespoons chopped fresh hot chile, or to taste

Combine all the ingredients in a food processor or blender and process until smooth.

TZATZIKI

Makes approximately 1 cup

1 6-ounce container of full-fat Greek yogurt (if using plain yogurt, use double the amount and strain until thick)
½ cup coarsely chopped peeled and seeded cucumber
2 tablespoons extra-virgin olive oil
Juice of half of a lemon
Kosher salt and freshly ground black pepper to taste
¼ cup stemmed, coarsely chopped fresh dill
2 garlic cloves, minced

Combine all the ingredients in a food processor or blender and process until well mixed. Transfer to a separate bowl, cover, and refrigerate for at least 1 hour, until thickened.

MALBEC BURGERS
with CREOLE MUSTARD TOMATO JAM

Makes 5 entrée-size burgers or 10 sliders Red wine goes beautifully with beef. And if I'm going to do a red wine recipe that speaks to a lot of people, it needs to be that universally loved set masterpiece: the hamburger. I like the fact that the wine not only breaks down the meat a little bit but also adds a nuanced flavor throughout the bite. It's not just when we drink the wine with the bite we're eating.

I came up with this dish while filming in New Orleans, and that is where the notion of Creole mustard came in. I love its creaminess, the big seeds, and that hit of vinegar and spice. In this recipe I use Alamos Malbec because of its great quality and its layers of big, interesting flavors (plus it's inexpensive! Score!). I have often loved the use of things such as tomato jam or confit in the place of ketchup on burgers. Here, we just use a nice, dark fruit-berry jam, which echoes the seediness of the mustard and brings out the fruitiness of the wine and the tomato.

FOR THE BURGERS

½ pound ground lamb

½ pound ground pork

½ pound ground beef (85% lean)

½ cup panko bread crumbs

½ cup finely chopped roasted tomatoes (see page 35)

⅓ cup finely chopped flat-leaf parsley

¼ cup finely chopped roasted garlic (see page 186)

3 tablespoons finely chopped sun-dried tomatoes

3 tablespoons finely chopped roasted red peppers (see page 107)

2 tablespoons finely chopped fire-roasted poblano chiles (packed in olive oil)

1 large egg

½ cup dry red wine, such as Malbec or Cabernet Sauvignon

2 teaspoons (packed) brown sugar

1½ teaspoons paprika

1¼ teaspoons crushed red pepper flakes

½ teaspoon sea salt

Olive oil, for pan searing

5 kaiser rolls for entrée-size burgers or 10 small potato rolls for sliders, split, toasted, and lightly buttered

BURGER TOPPINGS

Watercress leaves and sliced plum tomatoes

Creole Mustard Tomato Jam (recipe follows)

RECIPE CONTINUES

1 Preheat the oven to 375°F. In a large bowl, use your hands to combine all the burger ingredients except the oil and kaiser rolls. Form the mixture into 5 large (or 10 small) patties.

2 Heat an oven-safe pan over high heat until drops of water skitter across the surface. Add a quarter inch of olive oil and heat for 30 seconds. Sear the patties, working in batches if necessary, until browned on the bottom, about 3 minutes. Flip the burgers and brown the other side. Arrange the seared burgers on a rimmed baking sheet lined with aluminum foil.

3 Transfer the baking sheet to the oven and cook the burgers 5 to 7 minutes for medium doneness.

4 Place each burger on the bottom half of a toasted roll and top with watercress, sliced tomato, Creole Mustard Tomato Jam, and the top half of the roll. Serve hot.

CREOLE MUSTARD TOMATO JAM

Makes about 1 cup

⅓ cup fruity red wine, such as Merlot

⅓ cup crushed grape tomatoes

2½ tablespoons blackberry or raspberry jam

1 teaspoon sea salt

1 teaspoon freshly ground black pepper

1 teaspoon garlic powder

½ teaspoon onion powder

⅓ cup Creole or stone-ground mustard

In a small saucepan set over medium-high heat, combine the wine, tomatoes, jam, salt, pepper, garlic powder, and onion powder, stirring constantly, until thick and relatively uniform in consistency. Mash the tomato bits into the sauce. Transfer to a nonreactive bowl to cool. When cooled almost to room temperature, stir in the mustard.

SLOPPY 'ZO!

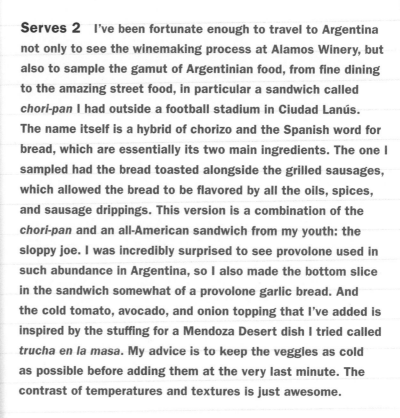

2 plum or vine tomatoes, halved and sliced into half-moons

½ red onion, julienned

1 avocado, peeled and cut into ½-inch chunks

Olive oil

1 tablespoon red wine vinegar

Sea salt to taste

1 head of garlic

½ large white onion, ¼ cup chopped finely and the rest julienned

2 garlic cloves, crushed

½ teaspoon crushed red pepper flakes

½ pound chorizo, casings removed

½ cup Alamos Cabernet Sauvignon (or your favorite Cabernet Sauvignon), plus ¼ cup for deglazing

1½ teaspoons paprika

1 12-inch baguette, unsliced

½ pound provolone, sliced as thin as possible

Serves 2 I've been fortunate enough to travel to Argentina not only to see the winemaking process at Alamos Winery, but also to sample the gamut of Argentinian food, from fine dining to the amazing street food, in particular a sandwich called *chori-pan* I had outside a football stadium in Ciudad Lanús. The name itself is a hybrid of chorizo and the Spanish word for bread, which are essentially its two main ingredients. The one I sampled had the bread toasted alongside the grilled sausages, which allowed the bread to be flavored by all the oils, spices, and sausage drippings. This version is a combination of the *chori-pan* and an all-American sandwich from my youth: the sloppy joe. I was incredibly surprised to see provolone used in such abundance in Argentina, so I also made the bottom slice in the sandwich somewhat of a provolone garlic bread. And the cold tomato, avocado, and onion topping that I've added is inspired by the stuffing for a Mendoza Desert dish I tried called *trucha en la masa*. My advice is to keep the veggies as cold as possible before adding them at the very last minute. The contrast of temperatures and textures is just awesome.

1 At least 1 hour in advance of making the sandwich: In a medium bowl, toss the tomatoes, red onion, and avocado together with 1 tablespoon of olive oil, the vinegar, and the sea salt. Cover and refrigerate for at least 1 hour. The veggie mixture should be very cold when put into the sandwich.

2 Preheat the oven to 375°F. Slice off the top third of the garlic head to expose the cloves, and place the head on a sheet of aluminum foil. Drizzle with 1 tablespoon of olive oil and wrap the garlic tightly. Roast for 45 minutes, or until the garlic is soft enough to squeeze out of the skins. Set aside for spreading on the bread.

3 Heat a nonstick pan over high heat until water drops skitter across the surface. Pour in enough olive oil to coat the pan generously. Add the julienned white onion (reserving the finely

RECIPE CONTINUES

chopped onion), the crushed garlic cloves, a pinch of sea salt, the red pepper flakes, and the chorizo. Cook until the chorizo is browned and the fat has rendered, about 5 minutes.

4 Add the ½ cup of wine to the pan and cook until nearly evaporated, stirring constantly and not allowing the meat to stick. Add the paprika and stir to combine.

5 Halve the bread loaf lengthwise and scoop out the inside of the top and bottom half. Brush the bread shells with olive oil and place them on a baking sheet. Use the back of a fork to spread equal amounts of the roasted garlic on each half. Top the bottom half with half of the provolone cheese. Toast the bread in the oven until the cheese on the bottom half is melted but not browned, approximately 3 minutes. Spoon the chorizo mixture on top of the melted cheese.

6 Add the remaining ¼ cup of Cabernet Sauvignon to the chorizo pan and deglaze over high heat. Add the finely chopped white onion and cook, stirring, until all the burnt bits on the bottom of the pan have been incorporated and the sauce begins to reduce and thicken. Spoon the onion mixture onto the chorizo mixture and top with the remaining slices of provolone.

7 Turn the oven to Broil. Slide the filled sandwich bottom under the broiler for approximately 2 minutes or until the cheese is melted and browned.

8 Spoon the cold vegetable mixture into the top half of the sandwich and close up the sandwich. Secure with toothpicks. Slice the sandwich into 2- to 3-inch portions and serve immediately.

SNACKS & SMALL PLATES

"APPETIZERS! IT'S WHAT YOU EAT BEFORE YOU eat to make you more hungry," said the rotund, misanthropic icon that is *South Park*'s Eric Cartman. And while he is not exactly the greatest sage in the land, certainly not about food—who could eat just the skin off of KFC and feel good about himself?—he's not entirely wrong in this case.

The small little bites we have before a meal are little smelling salts for our taste buds and salivary glands, slapping them awake and demanding attention. Speaking from my own experience, dishes like these are where chefs really get to flex their culinary creative muscles and let their freak flags fly. The diminutive size of these servings allows us to play with flavors and textures that might be overwhelming as an entrée but contribute a great bit of "whiz-bang" fun and pop as a part of an overall menu. Imagine wontons stuffed with all manner of things wild and wonderful, and you get the idea. These bite-size morsels of supercalifragilisticexpealidociousness are great for entertaining or to serve alongside cocktails or with a glass of wine. Served together, a selection of three or four could cater a gathering at your house or make a modern meal of crazy tapas. Dishes like these are the most fun to make, so let these straight up tasty morsels inspire you to create some of your own, whether you're Starvin' Marvin' the Ethernopian, Eric Cartman, or a chef named Chef.

SPICY TUNA ON CRISPY RICE

8 ounces sushi-grade tuna, minced

Dash of sesame oil

1 tablespoon Sriracha

2 green onions, white and green parts, finely chopped

1 tablespoon Japanese mayonnaise (like Kewpie)

2½ cups cooked and seasoned sushi rice

2 cups peanut oil

2 tablespoons sesame seeds

Serves 4 Most contemporary sushi restaurants serve some version or another of this recipe (Katsuya in LA has a particularly brilliant rendition), and the success of the dish depends entirely on the rice. I love the way the texture of creamy, spicy tuna contrasts with that of the crisp pan-fried rectangles of rice. If you can pick up some prepared sushi rice from your local sushi spot, this recipe is really easy to make and is an absolutely fantastic dish.

1 In a large bowl, mix together the tuna, sesame oil, Sriracha, green onions, and mayonnaise. Combine well.

2 Using your hands, shape the rice into rectangles approximately 2 inches by ½ inch. Make sure they are firmly packed, or they'll fall apart when you fry them.

3 In a 12-inch skillet, heat the peanut oil over medium-high heat until shimmering. Carefully add the rice rectangles, taking care not to overcrowd the pan and working in batches if necessary. Fry the rectangles until crispy and golden brown on all 4 sides, about 8 minutes total.

4 Drain the rice rectangles on a paper towel–lined plate. When cool enough to handle, top each rectangle with some of the spicy tuna mixture. Sprinkle with sesame seeds and serve warm.

SMOKED SALMON DILL DIP

1 bunch of fresh dill, stemmed and finely chopped

8 ounces cream cheese, at room temperature

1 tablespoon freshly squeezed lemon juice

1 teaspoon capers, plus more for garnish (optional)

¼ pound smoked salmon, minced

Paprika, for garnish

Makes about 2 cups This is a dish I make often as an appetizer for family gatherings. What's cool is the more I travel, the more this dish evolves, most notably after a recent trip to Alaska, where I tasted an incredible smoked salmon dip made by people who had caught their own salmon off the Kenai Peninsula. The thick-cut salmon fillets work best, because the flavor is more subtle. But don't be afraid to just chop up good ol' lox.

1 Chop the dill and measure ⅓ cup for the dip. Reserve another 1 tablespoon for serving.

2 In a medium bowl, beat the cream cheese with a wooden spoon until smooth. Add the lemon juice, ⅓ cup of dill, capers, and minced salmon and mix well. Chill for at least 1 hour and up to 2 days, covered with plastic wrap.

3 To serve, remove the plastic wrap and dust with the paprika. Sprinkle with the reserved chopped dill and additional capers if desired.

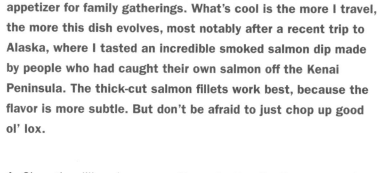

REUBEN MAKI

Serves 8 In a time when many of us are trying to avoid carbohydrates, this sushi-inspired sandwich roll captures the essence of a classic without weighing you down. There's no rice in this maki roll, but the melted cheese, sauerkraut, and Russian dressing are pure old-school Reuben, and the caraway seeds evoke the flavor of rye bread without the bread.

2 cups sauerkraut

1 cup Russian dressing

24 slices of deli corned beef

16 slices of Swiss cheese

1 large egg, beaten, for
  egg wash

2 tablespoons caraway seeds

¼ teaspoon coarse salt

1 Preheat the oven to Broil and set a rack in the top third of the oven.

2 In a mixing bowl, stir together the sauerkraut and Russian dressing.

3 Line a rimmed baking sheet with aluminum foil. Make 8 stacks of corned beef, 3 slices in each, and top each stack with 2 slices of cheese. Spread each stack with the sauerkraut-Russian dressing mixture and roll it into a cigar, securing the roll with toothpicks. Place the rolls on the prepared baking sheet.

4 Brush the rolls with the beaten egg wash and sprinkle generously with caraway seeds and salt. Place the baking sheet in the oven and broil for 2 minutes. Turn the rolls and cook 1 minute, or until browned.

5 Remove the rolls from the oven. Let the rolls rest for a minute, then cut each roll into 3 or 4 sections as you would a sushi roll. Serve hot.

EASY SUSHI

1 cup rice wine vinegar

¼ cup sugar

2 tablespoons salt

1 4-inch piece of kombu or kelp (optional)

½ cup sushi rice (or any short-grain white rice)

12 ounces (or more) sashimi-grade tuna

Wasabi paste, for seasoning and serving

Soy sauce, for serving

Pickled ginger, for serving

Serves 2 to 4 While I did not train in Japan, and I certainly acknowledge that I do not come from a sushi-making lineage, I do know the fundamentals—and, by all accounts, my sushi is pretty damn good for a honky. This recipe comes out of my limited experience as a sushi chef in New York and from my own kitchen. It makes for a perfect dinner if you're having someone special over—it's pretty easy and light, and you can even feed each other! Nigiri sushi, which is shaped by hand, is easier to make than rolls for novice sushi chefs, and you can make it with nearly any kind of fish you prefer. Use my recipe as a template, but feel free to freestyle. Above all, remember you are serving and eating raw fish, so it is best to purchase it from a fishmonger or a Japanese specialty shop you trust. Be sure to ask for the freshest "sashimi-grade" fish they have. Quality, freshness, and safety are things you cannot put a price on.

1 In a small pot set over medium-low heat, combine the vinegar, sugar, salt, and kombu (if using). Heat until the sugar and salt dissolve, then remove the pot from the heat and discard the kombu. Let sit at room temperature or in the refrigerator for at least 2 hours.

2 Cook the rice according to the package directions, either in a saucepan or in an electric rice cooker. You'll want the rice to be firm but a bit sticky.

3 When the rice is done, place it in a glass or wooden bowl. Add the vinegar mixture, and use a fork or a flat wooden spoon to cool down the rice and work in the liquid, spreading and turning the rice with a gentle chopping motion. Cover the rice bowl with a cloth towel and keep warm.

RECIPE CONTINUES

4 Thoroughly clean a cutting board and place the fish on it. Using a sharp knife, cut the tuna into thin slices about 1¼ inches wide. Don't worry about doing this as well as the sushi chefs you've seen—you won't be able to! Just try to slice the fish into the nicest, neatest pieces that you can. Using a small spoon or your fingers, dot each piece of tuna with a small dab of wasabi paste.

5 Wet your hands to start forming the very sticky rice into sushi-ready shapes. Using one hand as a cup, place a small portion of the rice (about 1 tablespoon) in your cupped palm, then use two fingers of your other hand to shape it into a long oval. The bottom should be flat and the top and sides rounded, but it needn't be perfect—just make somewhat symmetrical pieces so they all look about the same. Make as many rice ovals as you have tuna slices.

6 Gently lay the fish on top, wasabi side down (to help it stick to the rice), then press it firmly onto the rice. Serve with an additional dot of wasabi and a small bowl of soy sauce for dipping.

DEVILED SCOTCH EGGS

6 large eggs

1 cup all-purpose flour

2 large eggs, beaten

1 cup bread crumbs

1 pound bulk pork sausage, fully cooked and finely minced

Vegetable oil (enough to fill pot about 4 inches), for frying

¼ cup Hellmann's Light Mayonnaise

1 teaspoon white vinegar

1 tablespoon Colman's mustard

Kosher salt and freshly ground black pepper to taste

Serves 4 Deviled eggs have always been a staple at my family's Thanksgiving celebrations, and when perfectly executed, the creamy filling and paprika topping really create an explosive bite. This recipe is a flavorful reimagining of that classic hors d'oeuvre. I combine it with one of the rich and meaty classic bar bites from the United Kingdom: the Scotch egg, which is usually a medium-boiled egg coated in bulk sausage, breaded, fried, sliced lengthwise, and served with Colman's mustard.

1 Place the eggs in a single layer in a pot and cover them with water until there are 1½ inches of water above the eggs. Heat uncovered on high until the water begins to boil. Cover the pot and remove it from the heat. Leave the pot covered for 10 minutes, then remove the cover and run the eggs in the pot under cold water continuously for 1 minute. Remove the eggs from the pot and peel off the eggshells.

2 In one small bowl, place the flour. In a second small bowl, place the beaten eggs. In a third, medium bowl, combine the bread crumbs and sausage. Dip each boiled egg first into the flour, then into the beaten eggs, and finally into the bread crumbs.

3 In a deep skillet heat the oil over medium heat until shimmering, then, using a slotted spoon, place the eggs carefully into the oil, one at a time. Cook until golden brown on all sides, turning as needed. Again using a slotted spoon, remove the eggs from the oil and drain on a paper towel–lined plate until cool enough to handle.

4 Cut each egg in half. Remove the yolks to a medium bowl and combine them with the mayonnaise, vinegar, mustard, salt, and pepper.

5 Fill each of the fried-egg halves with a heaping spoonful of the yolk mixture. Serve warm.

HORSERADISH-PARMESAN ANGELS ON HORSEBACK

16 medium shrimp, peeled
and deveined

¼ cup grated Parmesan

2 tablespoons prepared
horseradish

1 large egg

8 slices of bacon, cut in half
crosswise

8 toothpicks

Vegetable oil, for shallow
frying

1 lemon, halved

Serves 6 to 8 Angels on horseback has been a cocktail party staple for decades, but my version improves on the original, if I do say so myself. Having tried the incredible grilled oysters at southern joints like Drago's in New Orleans, Wintzell's in Mobile, and Bowens Island Restaurant in Charleston, I've had the opportunity to experience the range of flavors that pair well with the grilled oyster. Here I apply that flavor knowledge to shrimp, pairing it with bacon's natural salty smokiness, a little bit of toasted-cheese creaminess, and some horseradish to cut through the richness.

1 Pat the shrimp dry with paper towels. In a small bowl, stir together the Parmesan and horseradish. In a separate small bowl, beat the egg until broken up. Dip the shrimp into the egg and then roll them in the Parm-horseradish mix to coat. Wrap each shrimp with a half slice of bacon, and secure with a toothpick.

2 In an 8-quart pot set over medium heat, heat about 2 inches of oil to 325°F on a deep-frying thermometer.

3 Add the wrapped shrimp and fry until the bacon is crisp, 5 to 7 minutes.

4 Drain the bundles on a paper towel–lined plate. Transfer to a warmed serving platter, squeeze the lemon over the shrimp, and serve hot.

UNSUNG MENU HEROES

Having traversed this country more times than I can count in search of the best of the best, I've encountered my share of local treasures, restaurants that are deservedly legendary for their sandwiches, their fried chicken, "Grandma's Coffee Cake," or whatever their specialty might be. But in more than a few of these places there are hidden gems on the menu that can outshine even the crown jewel if you're willing to stray from the beaten path and trust the locals. Here are few examples:

The Fried Chicken at Joe's Stone Crab (Miami Beach, Florida): Crispy, juicy, and it leaves your fingertips shiny, not greasy at all. Imagine the flavor of a good roasted chicken enveloped in a light-to-medium-thick golden-brown coating that has a satisfying crack when you bite into it.

The Grape Tomato Salad at Spumoni Gardens (Brooklyn, New York): Deceptively simple, this salad is all about quality of ingredients and execution. Crisp, slightly bitter mixed greens, grape tomatoes, dates, walnuts, matchstick-thin slivers of red onion, and four-inch-long triangular slices of ricotta salata (a somewhat salty sheep's milk cheese that has an oddly pleasant crumbly, chalky quality). The whole shebang is tossed in a vinaigrette that is basically invisible, just enough of it to make the leaves shiny. In a place where novel-thick slabs of Sicilian pizza and creamy spumoni have become the stuff of legend, this simple, yet incredible salad has inexplicably sailed under the radar. More for the rest of us!

Gargiulo Burger at Brennan & Carr (Brooklyn, New York): This place is as much a part of my youth as my Little League diamond and as much a part of me as my thigh (which still bears the scar of an accidental spill of their beef broth at age nine—and I'm not at all mad about that). Super-soft, thinly sliced beef, scalding-hot beef broth, seeded, gorgeous, sort-of kaiser rolls.

While their sandwiches range from hot roast beef on a dry bun to the sopping-wet, barely holding together KFJ (Knife and Fork Job; see "KFJ" Casserole Pie, page 113), they also serve this meaty masterpiece, a rare combination of juicy, wet sliced beef *and* a flat-top grilled burger with onions and cheese. This burger is at the very bottom of the menu and the name references the restaurant that its creators—waiters getting off work at the end of their shift—came from. It will rock your face off. Believe.

Tuna Tartare at Nick & Sam's (Dallas, Texas) / Tuna Tartare at Bern's Steak House (Tampa, Florida): These are steakhouses and, as is the case at most steakhouses, fish is an afterthought on the menu. It's what your weird cousin who majors in harpsichord orders. Not here. Bern's in Tampa takes advantage of that city's proximity to the water by serving this fresh, ruby-red tuna in their appetizers. Dallas's Nick & Sam's—a sexy, manly, and elegant steakhouse (intimate, yet HUGE) that oozes power—serves their tuna tartare (bear in mind, this is in freakin' Dallas) with jalapeño cotton candy (I'll pause while you take that in) that you melt over the tuna tartare with a special house-made ponzu sauce. Remember, man cannot live by beef alone; you need to order these items if you find yourself at either establishment.

Berkshire pork burger at Bark Hot Dogs (Brooklyn, New York): Look, I'm biased. The guys from my neighborhood hot dog joint made this for an event I hosted in Brooklyn for the New York City Wine and Food Festival, and it was love at first bite: succulent Berkshire pork shoulder and belly, spicy jalapeño slaw, pickles, and mayo on a pillow-soft roll. You may seriously tear up with the first bite. If you pair it with their fried Brussels sprouts, your tongue may jump out of your mouth and bitch-slap you for not eating there sooner.

MOCHIKO WINGS

FOR THE COATING

2 tablespoons oyster sauce or hoisin sauce

3 large eggs, beaten

½ cup soy sauce

2 tablespoons white sugar

2 teaspoons sea salt (preferably Hawaiian)

6 green onions, white and green parts, finely chopped

5 garlic cloves, minced

2 tablespoons all-purpose flour

¾ cup cornstarch

¾ cup mochiko (glutinous rice flour)

FOR THE WINGS

2 pounds chicken wings

1 cup vegetable oil or coconut oil

Sesame seeds

Sriracha, for dipping

Makes about 36 pieces Mochiko is a glutinous rice flour that I first saw used as a crispy, sweet coating for fish by Chef Mavro at the Hawaii Food and Wine Festival. It creates an incredible crispy exterior with a wonderful hint of sweetness that really enhances the flavor of the chicken while sealing in all the juiciness. Add some spice and a lot of sesame and you get a distinctly Polynesian flavor that is unique and delicious. If you like this coating, try it on fried fish fillets or even veggies.

1   In a large bowl, combine the coating ingredients and mix well. If the batter is thick, add a little bit of warm water to loosen it. It should be fluid enough to stir, but not watery. Stir in the chicken pieces, making sure to coat them evenly. Cover and refrigerate for at least 1 hour, or overnight.

2   Preheat the oven to 350°F. Line a rimmed baking sheet with aluminum foil and set aside.

3   Fill a large saucepan with the oil and set it over medium heat. Using a deep-frying thermometer, heat the oil until it reaches 375°F, or until it begins to shimmer.

4   While the oil is heating, take the wings from the refrigerator and let stand at room temperature for 10 minutes or so before frying.

5   Using a slotted spoon, carefully add the chicken to the hot oil in batches, cooking the wings until browned on one side, then turning them to brown the second side. Again using a slotted spoon, transfer the fried wings to the prepared baking sheet.

6   When all the wings are fried, place the baking sheet in the oven and bake for 15 minutes, or until cooked through.

7   Sprinkle the wings with sesame seeds and serve hot, with Sriracha for dipping.

SWEET AND SOUR TURKEY MEATBALLS

Serves 8 This is my grandma's recipe as reimagined by my mom. Grandma used to cook her meatballs in a gravy of chili sauce and grape jelly; I prefer to use a combination of cranberry sauce and barbecue sauce spiked with garlic. These meatballs are a great addition to a cocktail spread but can also be served over pasta or rice, or even in a bun.

2 pounds ground turkey breast

1 teaspoon dried thyme

Kosher salt and freshly ground black pepper to taste

2 large eggs, beaten

¼ cup (4 tablespoons) olive oil, divided

1 medium white onion, finely diced

4 garlic cloves, chopped

1 14-ounce can of jellied cranberry sauce (that solid cylinder of love)

1 14- to 21-ounce bottle of barbecue sauce (preferably a garlicky one)

2 tablespoons balsamic vinegar

1 In a large bowl, combine the turkey, thyme, salt, pepper, and eggs. Mix well and shape into about 32 meatballs about 1 inch in diameter.

2 In a large pot set over medium-high heat, heat 1 tablespoon of the oil. Add the onion and garlic. Cover and cook until the onions are soft and translucent, 5 to 6 minutes. Add the cranberry sauce, the barbecue sauce, the remaining 3 tablespoons of olive oil, and the vinegar. Bring to a boil, then reduce the heat to low so the sauce is just simmering.

3 Add the meatballs and cook for about 1 hour, turning occasionally. Transfer the meatballs and sauce to a serving bowl and serve hot with toothpicks.

PULLED PORK EGG ROLLS

24 egg roll wrappers

4 cups pulled pork (see Myron Mixon Pork Shoulder the Easy Way, page 126)

1½ cups prepared coleslaw

2 cups prepared barbecue sauce, preferably spicy

4 large eggs, lightly beaten, for egg wash

Vegetable oil, for deep frying

Prepared peanut sauce or hot sauce, for serving (optional)

Makes 24 egg rolls Of all the dishes I make for my family, this one is the most renowned. Buddy Merritt, a pitmaster from Arkansas, sent me some pulled pork as part of a barbecue care package, and I figured there had to be some other practical applications beyond just sandwiches for the smoky, savory shredded meat. When I threw some into egg roll wrappers with spicy barbecue sauce and coleslaw, I knew I was onto something. Since then, I have both pan-fried and deep-fried them with equal success. I highly recommend serving them with a peanut dipping sauce, though plain old hot sauce is totally okay, too.

1 Set a wire rack on top of a rimmed baking sheet and fill a small bowl with water.

2 Lay the egg roll wrappers on a clean, dry surface. Spoon about 3 tablespoons of the pork into the center of each wrapper, then top with about 1 tablespoon of coleslaw and a scant tablespoon of barbecue sauce. Using your fingertip, moisten all four edges of the wrapper with water. Fold two opposite corners in toward the center, then fold up the bottom edge and roll into a long, skinny cigar. Place the finished roll on the baking sheet and repeat with the remaining wrappers and filling. Brush the filled rolls with the egg wash.

3 Fill a large pot with about 4 inches of oil and set it over medium heat. Using a deep-frying thermometer, heat the oil until it reaches 375°F. Working in batches of 3 or 4 at a time, and using a slotted spoon, gently place the rolls into the hot oil. Fry until golden brown all over, turning occasionally, about 3 minutes. Again using a slotted spoon, remove the rolls from the oil and drain on a paper towel–lined plate. Serve hot, with peanut sauce or hot sauce on the side if desired.

GRILLED SHRIMP TACOS
with HONEYDEW SRIRACHA SALSA

½ honeydew melon, diced into small cubes

¼ cup Sriracha

4 plum tomatoes, diced

1 white onion, finely chopped

½ cup chopped fresh cilantro

1 jalapeño, seeded and finely chopped

1 tablespoon lime juice

4 garlic cloves, peeled

¼ cup olive oil, plus more for grilling

1 pound medium shrimp, peeled and deveined

12 small flour or corn tortillas

½ head of iceberg lettuce, shredded

Pico de gallo, for serving

Serves 4 Who doesn't love a good taco? In many cases, it's best to take the simplest approach to the protein, so your sauces can truly shine. Scott Romano, the amazing chef at the now-defunct Charlie Palmer at the Joule in Dallas, offered a charcuterie board that included balls of melon with a perfect blend of jammy sweetness and spice that blew my mind—he'd vacuum-packed them with Sriracha! I've incorporated that deceptive spiciness into the salsa here to make tacos. I think seafood-based tacos, like shrimp and fish, work best with fruit salsas, so I'm using the firm, crispy pop of grilled shrimp here.

1 In a sealable plastic bag, combine the honeydew and Sriracha. Add more Sriracha if the honeydew isn't completely coated. Press all of the air out of the bag, seal it, and refrigerate overnight.

2 The next day, in a large bowl, combine the tomatoes, onion, cilantro, jalapeño, lime juice, and marinated honeydew. Set aside.

3 Crush the garlic cloves and place them in a small bowl. Cover with the ¼ cup of olive oil and let sit for at least 30 minutes.

4 Preheat a grill (or a cast-iron skillet) until hot.

5 Pat the shrimp dry with paper towels, then brush them with the garlic olive oil. Thread the shrimp on skewers, then place the skewers on the grill. Cook for about 2 minutes, turn, and cook another 1 to 2 minutes, until just pink throughout. Transfer the shrimp to a clean plate. Remove and discard the skewers.

6 To assemble: Place a few shrimp in each tortilla and top with the melon salsa and lettuce. Serve while the shrimp are still warm. Pass the pico de gallo at the table.

HOMEMADE PIZZA

1 ¼-ounce package of active dry yeast

3 cups all-purpose flour, plus more to roll and shape the dough

1 teaspoon (packed) brown sugar

1 teaspoon salt

2 tablespoons olive oil, divided

Your choice of toppings

Makes 2 12-inch crusts One of my favorite movie quotes ever was uttered by Stephen Baldwin in *Threesome*: "Sex is kinda like pizza—even when it's bad, it's still pretty good." Being a New Yorker, I have been spoiled in the pizza department, but as I have traveled, I've learned that this is a sentiment shared in places like Chicago, Providence, and New Haven—legendary, respectively, for their deep-dish, grilled, and brick-oven varieties, like clams casino. Whichever style you like best, pizza is still the common denominator, and it's still awesome. Here is a simple approach to making 'za and maybe creating a style all your own.

Once you've got the trick of making great pizza dough under your belt, the sky is the limit as far as toppings go. I like to use caramelized onions, gouda, Cheddar, potatoes, and bacon.

1 Dissolve the yeast in 1 cup of warm water. Set aside for 15 minutes.

2 Fit a standing mixer with the dough hook. Combine the flour, sugar, and salt in the bowl of the mixer and, with the mixer on low speed, mix to combine them. With the mixer still running, add the yeast and 1 tablespoon of the oil. Continue to mix until the dough forms into a ball.

3 Lightly flour a clean kitchen counter or a large, clean wooden cutting board. Gently knead the dough to form a smooth, firm ball.

4 Grease a large bowl with the remaining 1 tablespoon of oil. Add the dough and cover the bowl with plastic wrap. Set aside in a warm area until the dough has doubled in size, about 1 hour.

RECIPE CONTINUES

5　Preheat the oven to 450°F. If using a pizza stone, place the stone in the oven to preheat as well.

6　Return the dough to the lightly floured surface and divide it into 2 pieces. Cover each with plastic wrap and let rest for 10 minutes.

7　Using your hands or a rolling pin, shape each dough ball into a large disk about 12 inches in diameter. Place the disk on a pizza pan or pizza peel if cooking on a pizza stone. Top as desired and transfer to the oven. Cook until the dough is browned, 8 to 10 minutes.

TOP IT OFF

Pizza crust is the perfect vehicle for just about anything you like to eat, and neither cheese nor tomato sauce has to be involved unless you want them to be. These are some of my favorite topping combinations, ranging from the classic margharita to the downright disruptive.

- caramelized onions, gouda, Cheddar, potatoes, and bacon (see page 89)

- brie, barbecued salmon, poached pear, and arugula

- pepperoni, white onion, fresh garlic, and black olives

- fresh mozzarella, vine-ripened tomato, and fresh basil

- spicy Italian sausage crumbles, crushed San Marzano tomatoes, and garlic

- grilled chicken, avocado, shredded iceberg lettuce tossed with mayo, tomato, and thick-cut bacon

BARBECUE-STYLE BRISKET FRIED RICE
with BLACK BEANS, CORN, GREEN ONION, and FRIED EGG

2 ears of corn

1 pound leftover cooked brisket (see Grandma's Home-Style Brisket, page 122) cubed

¼ cup vegetable oil

4 garlic cloves, minced

1-inch piece of fresh ginger, peeled and minced

3 cups day-old cooked white rice

1 tablespoon sesame oil

2 tablespoons soy sauce

1 12-ounce can of black beans, drained

⅓ cup thinly sliced green onions, light-green and white parts only

1 tablespoon unsalted butter

4 large eggs

Kosher salt and freshly ground black pepper to taste

Serves 4 Fried rice is perhaps the best use ever for old takeout rice, those stout little oyster pails of hardened starch that often end up completely wasted. I never get tired of coming up with new combinations. In this recipe I combined leftover brisket and eggs for a dish reminiscent of steak and eggs, plus the corn and green onions are evocative of a southwestern relish. However, this is simply one iteration; the variations are infinite. Feel free to throw in some of the Edamame–Roasted Corn Succotash (page 157), or add pineapple as they do at the Jitlada Thai restaurant in Los Angeles. Dale Talde, at his namesake restaurant in Brooklyn, loads his up with crabmeat. Feel free to emulate Hawaii's Side Street Inn and toss in char siu pork, Spam, or Maui onion. Have some cooked egg in the rice—or serve it loco moco–style, with a fried egg on top. Another way would be to crack the egg into the rice at the end and mix it in, as they do at Girl & the Goat in Chicago. Whatever version you come up with, enjoy the hell out of it!

1 Preheat the oven to 350°F.

2 Remove the outer leaves of the corn ear husks, but keep the inner leaves intact. Remove the silk and run each ear under water. Put the ears on a microwave-safe plate in the microwave and cook for 5 or 6 minutes, until softened. Transfer the corn to a rimmed baking sheet and roast for another 5 minutes, or until the corn is fully cooked. Remove from the oven and set aside to cool. Once cool, slice the kernels from the cobs into a large bowl.

RECIPE CONTINUES

3   In a wok or a large sauté pan, warm the brisket pieces over medium heat. Cook until the meat is slightly crispy and some of the fat has rendered in the pan, 3 or 4 minutes. Remove the meat with a slotted spoon and set it aside, leaving the rendered fat in the pan.

4   Turn the heat up to high and get the wok or pan very hot. Add the vegetable oil to the pan, followed by the garlic and ginger, and stir-fry for 1 minute, or until fragrant. Add the rice and cook, stirring frequently with a wooden spoon, until the rice is crispy, about 5 minutes. Stir in the sesame oil and soy sauce and cook for another 2 minutes.

5   Fold in the corn kernels and black beans. Cook and toss until warmed through, approximately 3 more minutes. Stir in the green onions just to combine, then transfer the fried rice to 4 warmed bowls.

6   Reduce the heat to medium. Add the butter to the wok or pan and, when melted, carefully crack the eggs into the hot pan. Season the eggs with salt and pepper and cook them sunny-side up until the whites are set. Place a fried egg on top of each bowl of rice. Serve hot.

SPANISH FLY
(PAELLA CAKES TOPPED WITH CRAB SALAD)

FOR THE CRAB SALAD

8 ounces lump crabmeat, picked over for cartilage or shells

⅓ cup diced celery

Freshly squeezed juice of half a lemon

¼ cup Hellmann's mayonnaise

¾ teaspoon Old Bay Seasoning

FOR THE PAELLA CAKES

5 tablespoons olive oil, divided

1 pound fresh chorizo sausage, casings removed and crumbled

1 6.5-ounce can of minced clams (juice reserved)

⅓ to ½ cup bottled clam juice

4 garlic cloves, crushed

2 medium onions, diced, divided

Kosher salt and freshly ground black pepper to taste

1 bunch of fresh flat-leaf parsley leaves, chopped

3 cups arborio rice

1 quart chicken stock

1 red bell pepper, seeded and chopped

Meat from 1 small rotisserie chicken, shredded

1 tablespoon paprika

Serves 8 I've dubbed this dish "Spanish Fly" because it is just that sexy. The refreshing crabmeat salad is a great counterpoint to the hot, crispy, and savory paella cake. Like the Spicy Tuna on Crispy Rice (page 71), this is another great example of cold, fresh seafood atop hot, crispy, savory rice, a contrast I just love.

1   In a medium bowl, combine all the crab salad ingredients and mix gently. Cover with plastic wrap and refrigerate until ready to serve.

2   In a large 4-quart paella pan or cast-iron skillet set over medium-high heat, heat half of the oil until hot but not smoking. Add the chorizo and cook, stirring occasionally, until the meat is browned, about 6 minutes. Using a slotted spoon, remove the chorizo from the pan and set it aside in a bowl. Leave the oil and drippings in the pan.

3   Drain the juice from the canned clams into a measuring cup and add enough bottled clam juice to make 1 cup.

4   Add the remaining oil to the pan along with the garlic, half the onions, a teaspoon of salt, and the parsley. Cook over medium heat for 5 minutes, or until the onions are translucent.

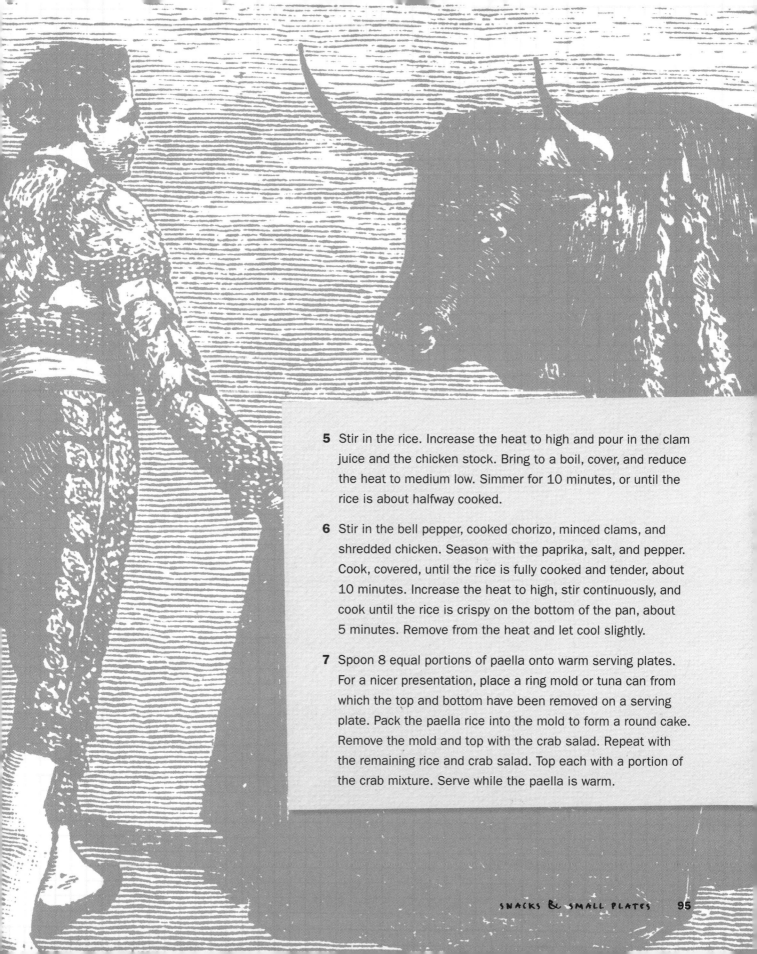

5 Stir in the rice. Increase the heat to high and pour in the clam juice and the chicken stock. Bring to a boil, cover, and reduce the heat to medium low. Simmer for 10 minutes, or until the rice is about halfway cooked.

6 Stir in the bell pepper, cooked chorizo, minced clams, and shredded chicken. Season with the paprika, salt, and pepper. Cook, covered, until the rice is fully cooked and tender, about 10 minutes. Increase the heat to high, stir continuously, and cook until the rice is crispy on the bottom of the pan, about 5 minutes. Remove from the heat and let cool slightly.

7 Spoon 8 equal portions of paella onto warm serving plates. For a nicer presentation, place a ring mold or tuna can from which the top and bottom have been removed on a serving plate. Pack the paella rice into the mold to form a round cake. Remove the mold and top with the crab salad. Repeat with the remaining rice and crab salad. Top each with a portion of the crab mixture. Serve while the paella is warm.

BAKED GOUDA
with SUN-DRIED TOMATO PESTO

1 8-ounce can of refrigerated
    crescent roll dough

½ cup pesto, prepared or
    homemade (page 107)

½ cup sun-dried tomato paste

1 tablespoon dried oregano

1 7- to 8-ounce round Gouda,
    wax removed, at room
    temperature

1 large egg, for egg wash

1 tablespoon olive oil

Serves 4 to 6 This recipe is one that my mother often made for her guests when I was a kid, and, with a little bit of a variation, it's what I served when I started to throw Super Bowl parties on my own. It's ridiculously easy and very impressive. The key is making sure the cheese is not ice cold—otherwise it will not melt all the way through! Feel free to improvise and experiment with toppings.

1 Preheat the oven to 350°F.

2 Remove the dough from the can, unroll it onto a lightly floured surface, and let it stand for 15 minutes or so to come to room temperature.

3 Roll the dough (or pat with your hands) into one big sheet large enough to enclose the cheese round. Spread the surface with the pesto and sun-dried tomato paste, leaving a 1-inch border around the sides. Sprinkle with the oregano. Place the cheese in the center of the pastry sheet.

4 Fold the dough over the cheese so it is fully encased. Place seam side down on a rimmed baking sheet.

5 In a small bowl, beat the egg with the olive oil. Brush the top of the dough with the egg wash.

6 Bake until the dough is golden brown, 15 to 20 minutes.

LATKES

1 flavorless vitamin C capsule (helps to keep the potatoes from browning while being prepared)

1 pound starchy potatoes, such as russets

1 large onion

1 large egg, lightly beaten

½ teaspoon salt

¼ to ½ cup all-purpose flour

¾ cup olive oil

Sour cream (or plain Greek yogurt) and applesauce, for serving

Makes 12 to 16 pancakes Jewish potato pancakes! The chosen hash brown! Applesauce's best friend! Next to seeing family, having time off from school, and getting the G.I. Joe helicopter and command center one memorable year, I consider latkes the best part of Chanukah. And don't relegate this dish to the holidays; topped with a dollop of sour cream, a slice of smoked salmon, and a little green onion, latkes are an incredible brunch dish.

1 Preheat the oven to 250°F.

2 In a large bowl, dissolve the vitamin C capsule in 2 table-spoons of hot water. Fill the bowl halfway with cold water.

3 Peel the potatoes and, using a box grater, coarsely grate them by hand. Place the shredded potatoes in the acidulated water as you go, then set the bowl aside for a couple of minutes. Drain the potatoes in a colander.

4 Coarsely grate the onion and add it to the colander with the potatoes.

5 Spread the grated potatoes and onion on a clean kitchen towel and roll it up jelly-roll-style. Twist the towel tightly to wring out as much liquid as possible. Transfer the potato mixture to a clean bowl and stir in the egg and salt. Mix in enough flour to create a thick batter.

6 In a 12-inch nonstick skillet set over moderately high heat, heat ¼ cup of the oil until hot but not smoking. Working in batches of 4 latkes, spoon 2 tablespoons of the potato

RECIPE CONTINUES

mixture per latke into the skillet, spreading it into 3-inch rounds with a fork. Reduce the heat to moderate and cook until the undersides are browned, about 5 minutes. Turn the latkes over and cook until the bottom sides are browned, about 5 minutes longer. Using a slotted spatula, transfer the latkes to a paper towel–lined plate to drain. Season with salt. Keep the latkes warm on a wire rack set in a shallow baking pan in the oven.

7 Repeat with the remaining batter, adding more oil to the skillet as needed. Serve hot or warm with sour cream, applesauce, or both.

VARIATION

GREEN-ONION CAKES, LATKE-STYLE, WITH DIPPING SAUCE

By changing up my latke recipe just a bit, you can approximate the green-onion pancakes served in Chinese restaurants. Grate the potatoes extra-fine, and replace the grated onions with chopped green onions. While not exactly the same as what you get in restaurants, they're way easier to make and delicious in their own right.

ROAST PORK AND BROCCOLI RABE DUMPLINGS

3 pounds pork loin

1 tablespoon extra-virgin olive oil

1 tablespoon dried sage

1 tablespoon dried thyme

1½ teaspoons kosher salt

½ teaspoon freshly ground black pepper

4 tablespoons (½ stick) butter

⅓ cup all-purpose flour

2½ cups pork or chicken stock

1 12-ounce package dumpling wrappers (with 48 wrappers), fresh or frozen and defrosted

1 small bunch broccoli rabe, de-stemmed and julienned (about 2 cups)

1 cup shredded extra-sharp provolone

Makes 4 dozen dumplings This dish was inspired by my favorite sandwich in the entire United States: the slow-roasted pork at Tommy DiNic's in Philadelphia's Reading Terminal Market, which took top honors on *Adam Richman's Best Sandwich in America*. The combination of slow-roasted pork with herbs, extra-sharp provolone, and broccoli rabe is the perfect balance of rich, salty, bitter, and spicy. Here I've reimagined it as a dumpling in which each bite delivers a punch of flavor. The dumplings make a great appetizer, or serve a few of them as an entrée.

1 Preheat the oven to 375°F.

2 Coat the pork loin with the olive oil, then rub it with the sage, thyme, salt, and pepper. Place the meat in a cast-iron skillet or other heavy-bottomed pan, and put the pan in the oven. Roast until the pork is fully cooked, about 45 minutes, or until the internal temperature of the meat registers 135°F on an instant-read thermometer.

3 Remove the roast from the oven and let it rest in the pan for about 20 minutes.

4 Remove the roast from the pan, reserving the pan juices. Wrap the meat in aluminum foil, and place it in the refrigerator to chill for about 10 minutes. (This will make it easier to slice it thinly.)

5 Put the cast-iron pan with the reserved pan juices over medium-high heat and add the butter. Using a wooden spoon, scrape up all the bits and pieces on the bottom of the pan. Then, using a wire whisk, whisk the flour into the pan a little at a time, and cook for 2 to 3 minutes. Finally, pour in the

stock a little at a time, whisking after each addition, until fully incorporated and there are no lumps in the gravy. Season to taste with salt and pepper, and keep warm.

6 Remove the pork from the refrigerator and cut it into thin, matchbox-size slices.

7 Place a few pieces of the pork into the center of a dumpling wrapper. Top with a little broccoli and shredded cheese (about a teaspoon). Using your fingertip, wet the outer edge of the dumpling wrapper with water. Fold the dumpling into a half-moon shape. While holding the dumpling curved side up, use your index finger and thumb to seal the dumpling. Start at one corner and work your way to the center. Then work from the other corner to the center. Make sure the dumpling is completely sealed. If there is too much filling and the dumpling cannot be sealed, remove the extra filling to prevent leakage during cooking.

8 Bring a large pot filled with water to a boil. Using a slotted spoon, carefully add the dumplings to the water and cook for 3 to 5 minutes. They are done when the dumpling skins are translucent and the dumplings have been floating for about 3 minutes. Again using a slotted spoon, carefully remove the dumplings from the pot and arrange them on a warm plate or platter.

9 Pour the gravy over the dumplings and serve hot.

HOT 'N' CRUNCHY AVOCADO & CHICKEN SALAD

FOR THE HOT 'N' CRUNCHY COATING

¼ cup slivered raw almonds

¼ cup sesame seeds

2 cups cornflakes

¼ cup sugar

1½ tablespoons crushed red pepper flakes

1 tablespoon salt

½ cup all-purpose flour

1 large egg, beaten

FOR THE SALAD

1 avocado, halved, peeled, and cubed

1 pound cooked chicken breast or tenders, shredded

1 tablespoon stemmed and chopped fresh dill

1 red onion, diced

1 tablespoon olive oil

½ cup Hellmann's Light Mayonnaise

Peanut oil, for frying

Serves 4 The Mighty Cone in Austin, Texas, is one of my favorite eateries on the entire planet. They do not call their food fried but rather "deep sautéed," and chicken is not the only thing that gets the deep-fried love they call "Hot & Crunchy"—a thin, flavorful, crispy coating made of cornflakes, almonds, chili de arbol flakes, sea salt, and sesame. Whole wedges of creamy-cool avocado get coated in their signature mixture before being combined with a slather of their "ancho paint" and Asian slaw. It all comes in a cone served with shrimp or chicken breaded in the same delicious "Hot & Crunchy" mixture. This salad has many of the same great flavors.

1 In a food processor, pulse together the almonds, sesame seeds, cornflakes, sugar, pepper flakes, and salt until the mixture has a coarse bread crumb–like texture.

2 Place the flour in a shallow bowl. In a second shallow bowl, place the beaten egg, and in a third, the hot 'n' crunchy mixture.

3 Roll the avocado cubes first in the flour, then in the egg, and then coat them with the hot 'n' crunchy mix. Arrange on a baking sheet to allow the coating to set.

4 In a large bowl, stir together the shredded chicken, dill, and onion. Add the oil and mayonnaise and stir well. Set aside.

5 In a large skillet set over medium-high heat, heat ¼ inch of peanut oil to 325°F on a deep-frying thermometer. Fry the avocado cubes until golden and cooked through, 2 minutes on each side. Drain on paper towels.

6 Divide the salad among 4 warmed bowls or salad plates. Top with cubes of fried avocado and serve immediately.

TORTELLINI, PINE NUT, SWISS, AND OLIVE SALAD

1 pound refrigerated cheese or herb tortellini (buy the best kind you can find)

1 tablespoon olive oil

¼ pound pancetta, diced

¼ cup pine nuts

½ pound Swiss cheese, cubed

¼ cup green olives, pitted and sliced

Serves 4 When my family went on picnics or to the beach, my father would pack a variation of this salad along for our lunch. Just the simple addition of pine nuts and chunks of Swiss cheese to the chewy, fresh tortellini, plus the bracing vinegary hit of fresh olives, makes this a great salad, hot or cold.

1 Bring a large pot of salted water to a boil. When the water is boiling rapidly, add the tortellini. Cook uncovered, stirring occasionally, according to package directions, or until the pasta floats to the top of the pot. Drain the pasta, put it in a large bowl, and toss it with the olive oil.

2 In a large skillet set over medium heat, cook the pancetta until crispy. Add the pancetta to the pasta, reserving the fat in the skillet.

3 Reduce the heat to medium-low, add the pine nuts to the skillet, and toast them in the pork fat.

4 Using a slotted spoon, transfer the pine nuts to the bowl with the pasta. Fold in the Swiss cheese and olives.

5 Serve warm, or cover and refrigerate to serve cold.

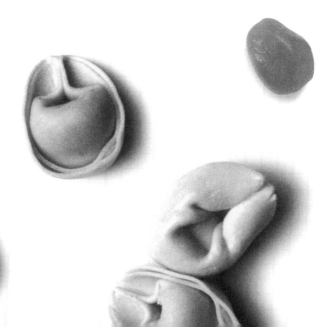

PESTO EGG SALAD
and ROASTED RED PEPPER

2 red bell peppers

¼ cup olive oil

2 garlic cloves, peeled

1 teaspoon crushed red pepper flakes

1½ teaspoons dried basil

6 large eggs, hard-boiled

3 tablespoons Hellmann's Light Mayonnaise

½ cup pesto (recipe below)

8 slices of pumpernickel or other sandwich bread, toasted

Serves 4 Texture- and flavor-wise, this sandwich is leaps and bounds ahead of the typical egg salad sandwich. Combining homemade roasted peppers and pesto with freshly made egg salad makes for an incredible sandwich that has the rich, unctuous qualities of cheese or pâté, with the punch of a fully loaded Italian hero.

1 Place the red peppers directly on the grate of your stovetop and turn the flame to high. Char the peppers, turning often, until blackened on all sides, about 5 to 7 minutes. (Alternatively, char your peppers under the broiler.) Transfer them to a paper bag, roll up the bag, and let the peppers steam for 15 minutes to loosen the skins.

2 When cooled, rub off the blackened skins from the peppers and discard the stems and seeds. Slice the peppers into strips and place them in a bowl. Cover with the olive oil and mix in the garlic, red pepper flakes, and basil. Cover and refrigerate overnight.

3 Peel the eggs and place them in a medium mixing bowl. Use a fork to mash them coarsely. Stir in the mayonnaise, adding just enough to make the mixture very creamy.

4 Dice the red pepper strips. Stir the pesto into the egg mixture and fold in the diced red peppers.

5 Serve the egg salad on the toasted bread.

PESTO

Makes 1¼ cups

2 cups packed fresh basil leaves

2 garlic cloves, peeled

¼ cup pine nuts

⅔ cup extra-virgin olive oil

½ cup Parmesan or pecorino cheese

Kosher salt and freshly ground black pepper to taste

1 In a food processor, pulse the basil, garlic, and pine nuts together until coarsely chopped. Slowly pour in the oil and process until fully incorporated and smooth. Remove to a bowl.

2 Stir in the cheese and season with salt and pepper. Use that day, or put the pesto in an airtight container and store in the refrigerator for a few days.

GRANDMA'S EGG SALAD

¼ cup olive oil

6 garlic cloves, chopped

1 large white onion, diced

8 large eggs, hard-boiled and peeled

Salt and freshly ground black pepper to taste

Serves 8 Egg salad was something I did not appreciate in my youth but came to love as an adult. Packed with caramelized, softened onions, this savory recipe does not contain nearly as much fat as its traditional mayonnaisey counterpart. It works hot or cold, in a sandwich or a wrap, and can be scooped into hearts of romaine for a low-carb option.

1 In a large skillet set over medium heat, heat the oil until shimmering. Add the garlic and onion, stir, then cover and cook until very soft, about 15 minutes. Mash up the warm garlic and onion as they cook until the mixture is a soft jam.

2 In a large bowl, use a fork to mash up the eggs into a soft spread. Add the mushy garlic-onion paste, season with salt and pepper, and stir until fully incorporated.

WHAT I LEARNED ABOUT FOOD FROM MY GRANDMA

My grandmother was born in Brooklyn. She's always had the same flaming-red (orangish) hair and has never lost her spark, her wit, her spunk, or her zest for life. And while Grandpa used to tease her, saying that what she most often made for dinner was "a reservation," Grandma could throw down. Granted, she does so less and less as the years go by, but she still knows how to bring the thunder in the kitchen.

Much as I did, she learned how to cook from her mother and grandmother. Her first recipe: eggs and onions. (We call it egg salad.) Her second was French toast. Grandma always had a facility with hearty breakfasts, especially old-school Jewish staples such as lox, eggs and onions, and kosher salami and eggs—one of my favorites (especially with Batampte Jewish yellow mustard—food of the gods, I tell you!).

It's funny where Grandma would cut calories and where she would use them. She always took pride in the fact that she used no mayo in her eggs and onions, but rather let the onions and the oil they were sautéed in provide the moisture. At the same time she often told me and my cousins, while offering us a morsel of decadent food, that it was "good for our coat." Apparently, Grandma operated under the assumption that I was a husky running the Iditarod.

When I asked Grandma what her cooking and food philosophy was, this was her response: "It has to be delicious, not too heavy to digest, and it has to be good enough to be your last meal."

Man, I love you, Grandma.

We who are about to dine, salute you.

DINNER

WHEN YOU THINK OF "COOKING FOR SOMEONE,"

these are the dishes you're probably thinking of. Entrées. The real-deal Holyfield with mass appeal and milk-fed veal. Dinner. Tablecloths, real cloth napkins, and the potential for more than one fork. Dear Lord, there may even be candlelight involved. And wine!

But breathe . . .

Take heart, culinary warrior.

Despite the pressure of making dinner for someone, or for a few people, I know you are more than equal to the task of hosting a dinner party or impressing a date. And just to make sure, I've studded this chapter with dishes, flavors, and techniques that incorporate the very best of the meals—dinners both expensive and cheap—that I've encountered all around the globe. I've also thrown in some tips and tricks from my own kitchen. The upshot is recipes that will blow you and your dining companions away, not only with their straight up tastiness but with their relative ease of preparation and eye-pleasing presentation. So, no fear and no bitchin', let's get into that kitchen. Unleash your culinary beast and create a great feast. Dinner is served. Bon appétit!

"KFJ" CASSEROLE PIE

2 tablespoons olive oil

2 large Spanish onions, halved and thinly sliced

Kosher salt to taste

4 cups beef broth

1 package of onion soup mix

2½ pounds sliced roast beef, cut into 1-inch strips

2 tablespoons unsalted butter, melted, divided

12 slider-size potato rolls

1 pound sliced Swiss cheese

Serves 12 I call this a "knife-and-fork-job" because it marries the juiciness of a French dip sandwich with the casseroles of my youth. The best part of eating a good French dip sandwich is that moment when the bread has taken on all the juice it can without disintegration—sort of the ephemeral cherry blossom of sliced beef, the green flash right as the sun dips below the ocean horizon. Brennan & Carr in Brooklyn creates this French-dip nirvana routinely, and it is their sandwiches that inspired this dish. If you ever get to Brennan & Carr, make sure to order the fries and a root beer in a frosted mug!

1 In a large pan set over medium-low heat, heat the olive oil for about 1 minute. Add the onions and cook, stirring infrequently, until they are brown and caramelized, about 35 minutes. Remove the pan from the heat and set aside.

2 In the same pan over high heat, combine the beef broth and the onion soup mix. Bring to a boil, then reduce the heat to a simmer. Add the slices of roast beef to the pan. Simmer the strips for about 10 minutes. Remove the roast beef slices to a bowl, reserving the broth.

3 Preheat the oven to 350°F. Grease a 9 x 13-inch casserole dish with 1 tablespoon of the melted butter. Slice the top halves of the rolls off and set aside. Place the bottom halves of the rolls in the casserole dish. Top with the caramelized onion and roast beef slices. Fill the pan with just enough beef broth to cover the beef. Top with cheese slices and then the top halves of the rolls. Brush with the remaining tablespoon of butter and cover with foil.

4 Bake the casserole for 25 minutes. Remove the foil and bake on an upper rack until the roll tops are golden brown, another 5 minutes.

5 Cut into individual sandwiches and serve hot.

LOCO MOCO

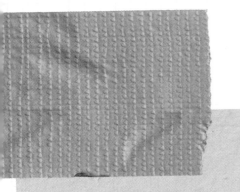

4 tablespoons unsalted butter, divided

2 tablespoons all-purpose flour

1½ cups beef broth

2 dashes of Worcestershire sauce

Kosher salt and freshly ground black pepper to taste

2 6-ounce hamburger patties

4 large eggs

2 cups hot, cooked white rice

Serves 2 In the pantheon of Polynesian comfort food, loco moco is without a doubt one of the most universally loved and widely attempted dishes. It's little more than rice, hamburger, gravy, and a fried egg. As my friend, Hawaiian chef Hiroshi Fukui, notes, though, while good rice is good rice, if you can make a good burger and good gravy—especially good gravy— you will have a good loco moco. So here is my homage to my *ohana* (family) in the Pacific. I hope you consider it *da ono kine grindz,* which loosely translates as "delicious eats."

1 In a small stockpot set over medium heat, melt 2 tablespoons of the butter. Whisk in the flour and continue whisking until you have a light-brown paste. Slowly and carefully pour in the broth while constantly whisking. Continue whisking until the flour is completely combined in the broth. Bring this gravy to a boil, reduce the heat to a simmer, add the Worcestershire sauce, and cook for an additional 5 minutes. Season to taste with salt and pepper.

2 Heat a large skillet over high heat until it is hot. Once the skillet is hot, place the hamburger patties in the pan and sear just until the juices start appearing on the top, about 3 minutes. Flip the patties over and cook for 2 minutes more, or until they reach your desired doneness. Remove the burgers from the pan and set aside.

3 Reduce the heat to medium and add the remaining 2 tablespoons of butter to the pan. Once the butter has melted, crack the eggs into the pan, being careful not to break the yolks. Fry sunny side up on low heat until the eggs are set, about 6 minutes.

4 To assemble: Place a small mound of rice on each of 2 warmed plates. Top with a burger, 2 fried eggs, and then pour the gravy over all.

CHIMICHURRI SKIRT STEAK
with BLACK BEANS

FOR THE CHIMICHURRI
(MAKES APPROXIMATELY 2 CUPS)

1 bunch of fresh flat-leaf
   parsley, stemmed and
   chopped

8 garlic cloves, minced

¾ cup extra-virgin olive oil

¼ cup red wine vinegar

Freshly squeezed juice of
   1 lemon

1 tablespoon diced red onion

1 teaspoon dried oregano
   (optional)

1 teaspoon freshly ground
   black pepper

½ teaspoon salt

1 2-pound skirt steak

3 tablespoons olive oil

Black beans (see page 118)

Serves 4 to 6 This is easily the dish that I most associate with South American—and in particular Argentinian—cooking. I had a girlfriend of Cuban heritage growing up, and she would make a hearty breakfasty dish with steak, fried eggs, sliced avocado, and black beans called *dia y noche*. The velvety starch of the black beans becomes a wonderful, gravy-like accompaniment to the crispy, buttery skirt steak. Add to it one of the most amazing Latin condiments—chimichurri—and you have a bright, garlicky, fresh, bracing counterpoint to the other rich and creamy elements of the dish.

1 Make the chimichurri: In a food processor, pulse the parsley until roughly chopped. Add the remaining ingredients and process for 1 minute or so, until all the ingredients are combined.

2 Preheat a large pan or skillet over medium-high heat until drops of water skitter across the surface.

3 When hot, add the olive oil and sear the steak on both sides, 2 to 3 minutes per side. (Take care to lay the steak down in the oil facing away from you, otherwise you run the risk of a very dangerous oil splatter.) If the pan is hot enough, the searing will bring the internal temp to the right place without additional cooking. However, if slicing into the meat reveals it's not yet done to your liking, place the pan in the oven at

RECIPE CONTINUES

350°F for a few minutes, checking often, until the desired doneness is achieved.

5 Serve hot with a side of black beans and the chimichurri.

BLACK BEANS

Serves 4 to 6

½ pound dried black beans

1 medium onion, diced

4 garlic cloves, crushed

Kosher salt and freshly ground black pepper to taste

1 The night before, rinse the beans thoroughly and then add them to a large pot of water. Cover and let soak overnight.

2 The next day, drain and rinse the beans. Discard the water in the pot. Return the beans to the pot and fill with water until the beans are just covered. Over high heat, bring to a boil. Reduce to a simmer, cover, and cook for 30 minutes.

3 Add the onion and garlic, and simmer, uncovered, until the onion is fully cooked, about 30 minutes.

4 Season with salt and pepper. Serve warm.

BONE-IN RIB EYE
SERVED OVER ARUGULA AND AVOCADO

2 bone-in rib-eye steaks
(1 to 1½ inches thick)

Kosher salt and freshly ground
black pepper to taste

1 tablespoon olive oil

3 cups arugula

1 ripe avocado, pitted, peeled,
and sliced

Maldon sea salt, for garnish

Serves 2 I am fortunate, being in the food industry, to have very generous friends with access to amazing foodstuffs. Pat LaFrieda and Mark Pastore of Pat LaFrieda Meats are a prime example—they gifted me with a ridiculously large box of their incredible steaks. Those guys know that bone-in rib eye is my absolute favorite cut because of its rich fat marbling and all the delicious flavor that comes with cooking meat on the bone. As far as really good steaks go, I generally think less is more. Salt, pepper, olive oil, and then careful monitoring of temperature usually produce an incredible steak. One night in Los Angeles, though, my manager had me over for dinner and served sliced steak over arugula and avocado, a presentation even I, who add avocado to just about anything, had never encountered before. The heat of the pan-seared meat wilted the arugula with the juices, creating a rich, light dressing for the greens and avocado. The combination of the bracing, peppery arugula, creamy-cool avocado, and the steak's unbelievable buttery, salty juiciness is just perfection.

1 Preheat the oven to 350°F.

2 Take the steak out of the refrigerator and bring it to room temperature before cooking. Season with salt and pepper just before searing.

3 Set a large cast-iron pan (big enough to hold both steaks) over high heat until it is screaming-hot. Add the olive oil and then sear the steaks on both sides, about 1 minute per side.

RECIPE CONTINUES

4 Transfer the pan to the hot oven and finish cooking the steak until it reaches your desired doneness, about 20 minutes for medium rare. You can also use a meat thermometer to check the temperature (140° to 145°F for medium rare); pull the steaks out of the oven 5 degrees before the desired final temperature. Transfer the steaks to a cutting board and let them rest for 5 minutes.

5 Mound the arugula on 2 plates, and arrange the avocado slices to one side. Slice the steaks, then reassemble them in their original form on the plates (this is how it's done in great steakhouses like Peter Luger's), placing it opposite the avocado. Drizzle the pan juices over the steaks and top each with a pinch of Maldon salt.

Know what **sauté** means?
High heat—fry with little fat.
In French, it means "jump."

You ready to **braise**?
Sear first, then cook in liquid.
Don't submerge the meat!

One must learn to **poach**:
Cook in simmering liquid.
Keep temperature low!

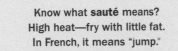

Need to **julienne**?
Cut the food into matchsticks,
Also called shoestrings.

You may need to **roast**:
Cooking with dry, diffused heat,
With oven or flame.

You must **caramelize**!
Browning sugars with some heat,
Some fat, and some time.

Sometimes you will **sear**:
High heat to cook the surface,
To get a nice crust.

Don't lose your **temper**!
Mix two delicate liquids.
Combine slowly—whisk.

GRANDMA'S HOME-STYLE BRISKET

4 pounds beef brisket

1 cup brewed black coffee, at room temperature

3 12-ounce cans of ginger ale

1 12-ounce can of Coke

1 cup soy sauce

1 teaspoon salt

½ teaspoon freshly ground black pepper

1 tablespoon garlic powder

1 large onion, sliced

Serves 6 to 8 When I asked my grandma for her brisket recipe, what you see here is how it came to me written out. Since then, I have always lovingly referred to the dish as "Grandma's Home-Style Brisket," even though in various subsequent versions of the dish I've made, I've added everything from oyster sauce and white balsamic vinegar to beer and other elements. However, this original version from my grandma will always produce a smoky, rich, tender brisket with loads of flavor. She's a great lady, and this is a great dish. I love her; you'll love her brisket. Serve this with roasted potatoes.

1 Place the brisket in a large sealable plastic bag. Pour in the coffee, 1 can of ginger ale, the Coke, and the soy sauce. Seal and refrigerate overnight.

2 Preheat the oven to 250°F.

3 Place the brisket in a large roasting pan, fat side up, with the marinade, salt, pepper, and garlic powder. Stir well. Cover tightly with aluminum foil.

4 Roast the brisket for about 2 hours, then remove the pan from the oven and add the remaining 2 cans of ginger ale. Cover the pan again with the aluminum foil and return it to the oven for another 90 minutes. Remove the aluminum foil and cook the brisket for another 30 minutes.

5 Remove the brisket from the oven and let it rest in the cooking liquid for at least 30 minutes before serving. To serve, place a slice or two of raw onion on a warmed platter with the brisket on top, then pour the flavorful pan juices over the whole thing.

HOME-STYLE CORNED BEEF AND CABBAGE

3 pounds corned beef brisket

½ teaspoon peppercorns

3 bay leaves

4 garlic cloves, crushed

1 head of cabbage (regular or savoy), cut into quarters

12 medium thin-skinned potatoes (such as Yukon Gold or red), rinsed

Serves 4 to 6 My original local watering hole in Brooklyn, O'Connor's Bar, used to serve free corned beef and cabbage every St. Patrick's Day, a tradition that made me proud to be both a Brooklynite and an O'Connor's regular. I'd become a devotee of corned beef and cabbage while living in Ireland after college. Traveling extensively throughout the Emerald Isle, I had a chance to sample this dish in its most traditional iteration. When executed well, it's a simple, delicious meal. Sadly, the pub has closed since the passing of the great Pat O'Connor, but his famous dish lives on.

1 Remove as much excess fat from the corned beef as possible, leaving just a little for flavor.

2 Bring a large pot of water to a boil (enough to completely submerge the beef). Toss in the peppercorns, bay leaves, and crushed garlic cloves. Add the corned beef and press it down with a heavy plate to submerge. Reduce the heat so that the beef simmers for about 3 hours. (Check for doneness by sticking a fork into the meat. The fork should insert easily.) Remove the meat to a cutting board to rest for at least 15 minutes, reserving the cooking water.

3 Place the cabbage and the potatoes in the water you cooked the beef in and bring the liquid to a simmer over medium-high heat. Cook until the cabbage is tender and the potatoes are fork-tender, 30 to 45 minutes.

4 Reheat the meat if needed and remove the obvious layer of fat before slicing against the grain. Place the sliced corned beef on a warmed platter, and pile chunks of the cooked cabbage and potatoes around the meat. Serve hot with some good rye bread or Irish soda bread, strong mustard, and some Guinness!

MAGNIFICENT MEATLOAF

1 pound ground beef

1 pound ground turkey

1 pound ground pork

2 tablespoons gochujang (Korean red chili paste)

3 or 4 green onions, light-green and white parts only, chopped

1 teaspoon liquid smoke

1 cup crumbled goat cheese

1 package of onion soup mix

¼ cup ajvar (an Eastern European roasted pepper and eggplant condiment)

Serves 8 Like everyone on the planet, I think my mother makes the best meatloaf. On the surface, this iconic dish seems like a pretty easy thing: seasoned meat pressed into a loaf pan. But done right, it can be so much more. Served hot or cold, a really great meatloaf is an invaluable addition to your cooking arsenal. Just make sure you don't overwork the meat, and keep the texture light and fluffy; otherwise it will be a brick of protein on your plate and in your belly!

1 Preheat the oven to 350°F.

2 In a large bowl, mix all the ingredients together until well combined. Press into a loaf pan.

3 Bake in the oven for 1 hour.

4 Remove the pan from the oven and let it cool a bit so the meatloaf fully sets. While still warm, slice and serve.

MYRON MIXON PORK SHOULDER THE EASY WAY

3 cups apple juice

1 cup distilled white vinegar

¾ cup sugar

¾ cup kosher salt

1 6- to 8-pound boneless pork shoulder/butt (blade roast)

1 cup pork rub, homemade (page 183) or store bought

Serves 10 to 12 I adore Myron Mixon. Truly. It is hard not to. He is unabashedly himself, wears short-sleeve shirts in the dead of winter like a Green Bay noseguard, can calculate the distance from anywhere in the world to his home in Georgia effortlessly, and loves his family, his country, and good barbecue. He has a ridiculously thick mane of his own hair. He is probably one of the best guys to get drunk with and is without question one of the best guys to be hungover with. And, most important, he has forgotten more about barbecue than most people will ever know. His pulled pork can be stuffed into anything from a plain hamburger bun to an eggroll or a ravioli. One bite, and I am sure you will say, as Myron himself so often does, "Dammit, MAN!"

1 Marinate the pork: In a large, heavy stockpot set over medium heat, whisk together the apple juice and the vinegar. Whisking continuously, pour in the sugar and salt. Continue whisking until the sugar and salt are completely dissolved, but do not allow the mixture to come to a boil. When the sugar and salt are completely dissolved, remove the pot from the heat and let it cool completely.

2 Place the pork shoulder in a large aluminum baking pan. Add the cooled marinade, cover the pan, and let the pork marinate in the refrigerator for at least 1 hour before cooking or, if you can, overnight.

3 Roast the pork in a smoker: Heat the grill to 550°F and close the lid. Wait at least 15 minutes, until the temperature has lowered to about 300°F.

4 Remove the meat from the marinade. (Discard the marinade.) Pat the meat dry with paper towels and season well with the pork rub.

5 Place the roast back into the aluminum pan, fat-side down and uncovered, and transfer it to the smoker for about 2½ hours total. The pork is ready when it reaches an internal temperature of 150°F.

6 Remove the pork from the smoker, cover it with aluminum foil, and let it rest for 30 minutes (it will continue to cook when it's off the heat, raising the internal temperature to the recommended 160°F). After the pork has rested, pull it, chop it, or slice it as you wish.

Roasting the pork in the oven: Preheat the oven to 300°F. Remove the meat from the marinade. (Discard the marinade.) Pat the meat dry with paper towels and season well with the pork rub. Place the roast in an aluminum pan, fat-side down and uncovered, in the oven for about 2½ hours. The pork is ready when it reaches an internal temperature of 150°F. Remove the pork from the oven, cover with aluminum foil, and let it rest for at least 30 minutes and as long as 1 hour (it will continue to cook when it's off the heat, raising the internal temperature to the recommended 160°F). After the pork has rested, pull it, chop it, or slice it as you wish.

MAPLE-GLAZED PORK BELLY POUTINE
and SWEET POTATO FRIES

3 pounds pork belly

1 tablespoon ground cinnamon

1 teaspoon freshly grated nutmeg

1 tablespoon ground allspice

1 tablespoon kosher salt

1 tablespoon olive oil

1 cup maple syrup, plus more as needed

1 cup apple juice

1 cup pumpkin puree

1 package of frozen sweet potato fries, cooked per the package instructions

1 cup fresh burrata cheese, cubed or separated into chunks

Serves 6 The direct inspiration for this dish comes from an amazing restaurant in Portland, Maine, called Nosh. The executive chef, a brilliant CIA graduate, took Canada's comfort-food staple, poutine—most commonly gravy and cheese curds atop French fries—and made it his own by including the decadent, melt-in-your-mouth pork belly. Bringing up a little bit more of an autumnal kind of holiday flavor, I use sweet potato fries and gravy made from pork drippings, apple juice, the mild, fragrant, oniony flavor of melted leeks, and pureed pumpkin. Instead of the traditional cheese curds, which are not always easy to come by (and sometimes prove to be a little too chewy and rubbery for a dish that needs melting), I am using an Italian classic: milky, creamy, slightly stretchy burrata. It's a Canadian dish, by way of Maine, Plymouth Rock, and Italy.

1 Preheat the oven to 250°F.

2 Rub the pork with the cinnamon, nutmeg, allspice, and salt.

3 In a large cast-iron pan over medium heat, heat the olive oil. Once the oil is shimmering, sear the pork belly on all sides until browned all around, about 7 minutes. Remove the pork from the heat and pour 1 cup of the maple syrup over the pork belly; cover the pan with aluminum foil and place it in the oven.

RECIPE CONTINUES

4 Cook the pork for 20 minutes. Remove the pan from the oven, uncover, then brush the pork with the pan juices, and return it to the oven. Continue cooking, glazing every 20 minutes with additional maple syrup, if needed, for another 2 hours.

5 Remove the pork from the pan and set it aside to rest. Pour the pan juices into a measuring cup. Place the pan over medium heat and add the apple juice. Heat the liquid, scraping up the pork pieces from the bottom of the pan, until the apple juice begins to boil. Stir in the pumpkin puree and enough of the pan juices to create a gravy-like consistency. Cook for a few minutes to heat through. Thin it a bit with additional apple juice if necessary.

6 Set the oven to Broil. Cut the pork into cubes.

7 In a large oven-safe dish, layer the precooked fries evenly. Top the fries with the pork cubes, then the burrata, and then the pumpkin–apple juice gravy. Place the pan under the broiler and broil for 2 to 3 minutes, until the cheese has melted. Serve hot.

NATIVE SON

For someone who's grown up in Brooklyn and has always called it home, it's kind of crazy when all of the sudden the entire world knows where it is, what it is, and starts sporting its name on T-shirts and messenger bags. Before Brooklyn was the land of artisanal chocolates and cocktail bars staffed by tattooed, bearded men dressed like nineteenth-century farmers—and when Bushwick was a place few traveled to and fewer returned from—it was the next stop for immigrant families leaving the overcrowded squalor of the Lower East Side of Manhattan. Brooklyn really represented the melting pot in its purest form.

The Brooklyn I grew up in was color blind. You could end up eating with a Sicilian family one night, a Jamaican family the next. Moms of every ethnicity would exchange recipes at playgrounds or while waiting to pick kids up from school, and mine was no different. Dinner might be the hearty Eastern European stew known as cholent one night, then escarole, sausage, and beans the next. And because Brooklyn was infinitely more affordable then than it is now, many first-generation immigrant families opened restaurants or grocery stores selling authentic tastes of their homelands for very cheap. It was not uncommon for a group of us kids, a veritable Benetton ad of different backgrounds, to go out together after school for Syrian shawarma, knishes, Chinese roast-pork buns, falafel, or Jamaican beef patties. It didn't feel like "going local" or "eating ethnic"—it was Brooklyn. We were Brooklyn, the County of Kings, descendants of those who dodged trollies, rooted for Jackie, Pee Wee, and Roy, and rode the Cyclone at Coney Island. We were rough, ready, and rapacious; we saw the Manhattan prep school kids as soft, marks, snobs. We loved cannoli, kibbeh, and pierogi in equal measure and knew where to get the best ones. We knew just enough Russian, Italian, or Greek to get by and get what we wanted. We ate real Russian food in Little Odessa. The Russian Tea Room could kiss our ass. (By the way, having eaten there recently, it still can—OVERRATED AND OVERPRICED.)

Now, while I take pride that the world has turned its gaze toward the hometown I love, today it's a different eating scene. Authentic Old World has been replaced by new goods in "old" style. Fancy new flavors, served in Mason jars and from menus with old-timey print. Talented chefs no longer consider cooking in the world across the bridge as slumming-it, but rather as a badge of honor. And the neighborhoods one would never walk into without some means of self-defense now attract leather elbow–patched denizens armed with hand sanitizer, Stevia, and a well-thumbed copy of the *Zagat* guide or the *Economist*.

As much as I miss the old—and most authentic Brooklynites do—I welcome the new, because at the end of the day, Brooklyn is getting the respect it has always deserved. I'm not just talking about silly stuff like the darn MTV Video Music Awards happening two blocks from my house (which sucked), but that we are a destination. We are valid and vibrant, and we will graffiti, switchblade, and break-dance all up on your taste buds and rock your palate in the way only BK can. As Mos Def says, "Manhattan keep on making it, Brooklyn keep on taking it." You want good food, real people, and real life—"B-to-the-R-to-the-O-the-O-K / L-Y-N is the place where I stay." Root to the fruit—I eat here, I live here, I'll die here, and I wouldn't have it any other way. If you don't know, now ya know, homie.

FRENCH FARMHOUSE–STYLE SIMPLE ROASTED CHICKEN

1 whole free-range, organic chicken (about 3½ pounds)

1 tablespoon herbes de Provence

Kosher salt and freshly ground black pepper

1 cup plus 1 tablespoon extra-virgin olive oil

Freshly squeezed juice of 1 Meyer lemon

3 garlic cloves, minced

1 cup chopped fresh parsley

1 cup chopped fresh cilantro

Serves 4 Long ago, my mom dated a guy from a region called the Dordogne located in the hinterlands between France, Germany, and Switzerland. He was partial to classic French or Swiss country fare: radishes with butter, asparagus with mayo, and so on. In addition to teaching me how to make a really solid vinaigrette, he shared his mother's philosophy: a good cook can make a wonderful roast chicken without a ton of ingredients and can keep the skin nice and crispy without sacrificing the moistness of the meat. My chef friend Spike Mendelsohn from Washington, DC, makes an elegant and simple version using only salt, pepper, olive oil, and maybe some fresh herbs and says it's one of his favorite things to cook. This version doesn't use much more than that. Here again is proof that if you stick to the basics and really focus on preparation, you don't need fancy sauces to make a truly delicious and hearty classic dish.

1 Preheat the oven to 425°F.

2 Wash the chicken and thoroughly dry it with paper towels. Using kitchen shears, cut out the backbone of the chicken by cutting up the back on one side of the backbone and then cutting up the back on the other side. Discard the backbone. Season the chicken with the herbes de Provence, salt, and black pepper.

3 Place the chicken, skin side up, in a Dutch oven. Drizzle 1 tablespoon or so of olive oil over the bird. Place the pan in the oven, uncovered, and roast for 35 minutes.

4 While the chicken is roasting, in a small bowl combine the

RECIPE CONTINUES

remaining 1 cup of olive oil, lemon juice, garlic, parsley, and cilantro. Stir to combine.

5 Remove the chicken from the oven, cover it with the seasoned olive oil and herbs, then return it to the oven for an additional 15 minutes. The chicken is done when the juices from the thigh run clear or it reaches an internal temperature of 155°F, as measured with a meat thermometer.

CHICKEN MARSALA

4 skinless, boneless chicken breasts

1 cup buttermilk

½ cup grated Parmesan cheese

1½ teaspoons garlic powder

¼ teaspoon kosher salt

A pinch of freshly ground black pepper

½ cup all-purpose flour

1 large egg, beaten

2 tablespoons extra-virgin olive oil

3 ounces prosciutto, thinly sliced

6 ounces cremini or fresh porcini mushrooms, stemmed and halved

⅓ cup sweet Marsala wine

⅓ cup chicken stock

1½ tablespoons unsalted butter

Serves 4 This amazingly easy version of a classic fine dining recipe comes courtesy of the best chef I know on planet Earth: my mom. I recommend this one for any college dudes wishing to impress or bachelors in their first apartment. The flavor is amazing, and it's as good cold in a hero as it is hot on the plate served with a vegetable side. It's also a great illustration of how flavor can be added with a slight variation on the traditional seasoning one might use to dredge the cutlets.

1 Place the chicken breasts on a cutting board and cover with plastic wrap. Pound with a flat meat mallet until they are uniformly about ¼ inch thick. Place the chicken in a shallow baking dish and add the buttermilk. Turn to coat the chicken cutlets, then cover the dish and refrigerate overnight.

2 Combine the Parmesan, garlic powder, salt, and pepper on a plate or in a shallow bowl. Put the flour and beaten egg into two separate bowls. Dredge each chicken breast in the flour, then in the beaten egg, and then in the seasoned cheese, placing each as it's done on a platter or baking sheet to set.

3 In a large skillet set over high heat, heat the olive oil. Slip the coated chicken breasts into the pan and fry for 5 minutes. Flip them over and cook until they are golden brown, about 3 minutes. Transfer the chicken to a platter and loosely cover to keep warm.

4 Lower the heat to medium and add the prosciutto to the pan. Cook for 1 minute, then add the mushrooms and sauté until they are nicely browned and their moisture has evaporated, about 5 minutes. Pour the Marsala wine into the pan and bring to a boil. Cook until thick, about 3 minutes. Add the chicken stock and simmer for 2 minutes until somewhat reduced and thickened. Stir in the butter and heat until just melted. Return the chicken to the pan and cook for 2 more minutes to heat the chicken through. Season to taste with additional salt and pepper as desired and serve hot.

PICK A PROTEIN!

At some restaurants—including many Asian ones—once you select a dish you can have it made with your choice of protein: beef, chicken, shrimp, fish, or vegetable. If you'd rather begin by picking your protein, here are my nominees for the best in each category.

BEEF

SHORT RIB KARE KARE
Talde, Brooklyn, New York

SPECIAL CHATEAUBRIAND
Bern's Steak House, Tampa, Florida

THE RICHWICH
Chaps Pit Beef, Baltimore, Maryland

MEATBALL PIZZA
Bob & Timmy's Grilled Pizza, Providence, Rhode Island

BÁHN MÌ FRENCH DIP
The Pig and the Lady, Honolulu, Hawaii

CHICKEN

FRIED CHICKEN
Gus's Fried Chicken, Memphis, Tennessee

CHICKEN SANDWICH
Son of a Gun, Los Angeles, California

YARDBIRD SANDWICH
Slows Bar B Q, Detroit, Michigan

CHICKEN ROLL
Carmine's Pizzeria, Brooklyn, New York

ROASTED CHICKEN
RPM Italian, Chicago, Illinois

PORK

WHOLE HOG BARBECUE
Pete Jones BBQ, Jones Skylight Inn, Ayden, North Carolina

CRYING TIGER PORK
Jitlada, Hollywood, California

BABY BACK RIBS
Henry's Hi-Life, San Jose, California

SLOW-ROASTED PORK
Brasa Premium Rotisserie, Minneapolis, Minnesota

OHSAM BOKKEUM
Miss Korea BBQ, New York City, New York

FISH

TOPPING NIGIRI
Sushi of Gari, New York City, New York

STRIPPED BAZE (STRIPED BASS)
Katsuya, Hollywood, California

OPAKAPAKA
Side Street Inn, Honolulu, Hawaii

PESCADO EMPAPELADO
Azul Tequila, Austin, Texas

BLACK DRUM
Borgne Restaurant, New Orleans, Louisiana

SHRIMP

GIOVANNI'S SCAMPI OR HOT & SPICY
Giovanni's Shrimp Truck, Kahuku, Hawaii

HOT & CRUNCHY SHRIMP CONE
The Mighty Cone, Austin, Texas

BBQ SHRIMP
Deanie's, Metairie, Louisiana

SURF AND TURF PO'BOY
Parkway Bakery & Tavern, New Orleans, Louisiana

SHRIMP PO'BOY
Domilise's, New Orleans, Louisiana

GREEN CURRY WITH SHRIMP
Song, Brooklyn, New York

AND FOR NON-MEAT-EATERS, MEAT SUBSTITUTES:

SQUASH BLOSSOM QUESADILLA
Taco Bus, Tampa, Florida

CRISPY VEGGIE CHICKEN NUGGETS
Vegetarian Palate, Brooklyn, New York

HEART OF PALM CRAB CAKES
Crossroads, Los Angeles, California

TEMPEH REUBEN
Sage Vegan Bistro, Culver City, California

NACHOS WITH VEGAN CARNE MOLIDA
The V-Spot, Brooklyn, New York

VEGGIE CHILI

3 tablespoons olive oil

1 large yellow onion, diced

6 garlic cloves, chopped

Kosher salt and freshly ground black pepper to taste

1 12-ounce package of Lightlife Smart Ground Original vegan crumbled beef

2 tablespoons chili seasoning

1 15-ounce can of chickpeas

1 15-ounce can of black beans

1 10-ounce can of Ro-Tel Diced Tomatoes & Green Chilies

2 16-ounce jars of red salsa (either 2 medium-spicy or 1 hot plus 1 mild; avoid fruit or verde salsas)

Cholula (or your favorite hot sauce) to taste

1 cup shredded Cheddar cheese (optional)

1 avocado, pitted and sliced

2 cups plain Greek yogurt (or sour cream)

Serves 4 This is another recipe from Mom that has undergone several changes since I got my hands on it. Although there is no meat in this recipe, I treat the meat substitute like the real thing and brown it before adding the remaining ingredients. It's an extra step, but since the rest of the recipe is basically opening cans and jars and adding stuff in the right order, then allowing the flavors to combine while not letting anything burn, I think it's worth the extra bit of effort. This chili makes a great topping for nachos, hot dogs, or burgers. It's a great recipe for bachelors and students, and it's easy to make a large batch very cheaply (it will keep in the refrigerator or freezer for a long time).

1 Set a Dutch oven or stockpot over medium-high heat. Add the olive oil and heat until hot, but not smoking. Add the onion and garlic and cook, stirring occasionally, until translucent, about 3 minutes. Season the vegetables with salt and pepper. Stir in the Smart Ground and sauté until browned, about 3 minutes. It should have the consistency of taco filling.

2 Add the chili seasoning, chickpeas and beans (with their liquids), Ro-Tel, and salsa. Stir everything to combine. Add hot sauce to taste. Increase the heat to high. Bring the chili to a boil, then reduce the heat and simmer for about 1 hour. Adjust the seasoning before serving.

3 Serve the chili hot in bowls topped with sprinklings of cheese, slices of avocado, and spoonfuls of yogurt.

EASY LEMON BUTTER SALMON

1 2-pound skinless salmon fillet

1 cup white wine

½ cup freshly squeezed lemon juice

2 tablespoons olive oil

4 tablespoons cold unsalted butter, divided into tablespoon-size pieces

1 lemon, sliced into disks

Serves 4 Lemon and butter are two of salmon's best friends. In the best fish restaurants, among which I would sure number Street and Co. in Portland, Maine, preparation maintains the essence of the fish. (This is actually Street and Co.'s motto and appears on their website as well.) Good salmon, like Coho River or wild Alaskan sockeye, has loads of flavor. Lemon and seafood go together like hugs and kisses, serving to heighten the flavor and freshness of the seafood. The butter adds a really lovely, velvety texture, but don't overdo the dairy or it will overpower the fish!

1 In a shallow bowl, cover the salmon with the wine and lemon juice. Cover and refrigerate for 30 minutes (no more than that, or it will "cook" like ceviche and become mushy).

2 Preheat the oven to 350°F.

3 Brush a roasting pan with the olive oil. Pat the salmon dry (discard the marinade) and place it in the roasting pan. Dot the salmon with the cold butter and lemon slices. Cover the pan with aluminum foil and bake the salmon for 20 minutes. Uncover and cook for another 5 minutes. Serve hot.

BARBECUED SHRIMP

Serves 4 to 6 Barbecued shrimp is one of the most ubiquitous seafood dishes in New Orleans, and every place does it differently. My first formal exposure to this universal crowd-pleaser was when shooting *Man v. Food* at a New Orleans legend, Deanie's in Bucktown. The simple use of a well-made compound butter, great seafood, and one of my absolute favorite flavors in the entire vegetable realm—green onion—makes this dish extraordinary. Make sure to have plenty of great bread on hand to soak up the sauce. Think crusty baguette if you can't get Louisiana's famous French bread made by the Leidenheimer Baking Company!

2 cups (4 sticks) unsalted butter, softened, divided

2 tablespoons paprika

½ teaspoon dried thyme

½ teaspoon onion powder

½ teaspoon garlic powder

¼ teaspoon freshly ground black pepper

2 tablespoons cayenne pepper

1 tablespoon kosher salt

3 pounds large shell-on shrimp

Freshly squeezed juice of 1 lemon

1 bunch green onions, white and green parts sliced on a diagonal into inch-long pieces

4 garlic cloves, minced

1 Make the Cajun butter: In a food processor, pulse 1 cup (2 sticks) of the butter with the paprika, thyme, onion powder, garlic, and black pepper. Blend until combined. Scrape the butter into a bowl, cover, and refrigerate for at least 3 hours.

2 Make the cayenne butter: Clean out the food processor and add the remaining 1 cup of butter, the cayenne pepper, and the salt. Blend until combined. Scrape the butter into a bowl, cover, and refrigerate for at least 3 hours.

3 Heat a cast-iron skillet over high heat. Add half of the Cajun butter; once the butter has melted, add the shrimp, the remaining Cajun butter, the lemon juice, the green onions, and the garlic. Cook until the shrimp turn pink, about 1 minute. Reduce the heat to medium and stir in ⅔ of the cayenne butter. Cook until the shrimp are fully cooked and most of the butter has melted.

4 With a slotted spoon, transfer the cooked shrimp to a warmed plate. Increase the heat under the pan to high and add the remaining cayenne butter. Scrape the pan drippings together while the butter melts. Pour the pan sauce over the shrimp and serve with plenty of crusty bread.

LINGUINE
with ARUGULA, SAUSAGE, TOASTED MACADAMIA NUTS, and SHRIMP

1 pound medium shrimp, peeled and deveined

1 cup Italian dressing

Kosher salt, for cooking the pasta

1 pound dried linguine

1 cup macadamia nuts

1 tablespoon olive oil

1 pound Italian sausage links, pierced in several places with a fork

4 tablespoons unsalted butter, divided

1 bunch of arugula

Cracked black pepper

Finely grated pecorino Romano cheese to taste

Serves 4 I love noodle dishes in general, whether it be ramen noodles, pad Thai, or the ubiquitous Hawaiian saimin (noodle soup). Ingredient-wise, this recipe looks to my favorite place on earth—Hawaii—for the buttery crunch and awesome fresh pop of seafood and macadamia, but I've also added flavors from Italian pasta dishes: bitter greens like arugula and, of course, Italian sausage. The fats from the nuts and the sausage end up creating a sauce unto themselves and a wonderful velvety coating for each noodle.

1 In a medium bowl, toss the shrimp with the Italian dressing; cover and refrigerate for 30 minutes.

2 Bring a large pot of heavily salted water to a boil over high heat. Add the linguine and cook until slightly al dente (it should be a bit chewy). Reserve 1 cup of the cooking water, then drain the pasta in a colander.

3 Heat a heavy cast-iron pan over medium heat until hot. Add the macadamia nuts and toast them until browned (but don't burn them!). Remove the nuts to a plate and set aside.

4 Increase the heat to high and add the olive oil to the pan. Once the oil is hot, add the sausage and sauté until cooked through, about 8 minutes, adding more olive oil if necessary. Remove the sausage from the pan, slice it into 1-inch pieces, and set aside.

RECIPE CONTINUES

5 Reduce the heat to medium and add 2 tablespoons of the butter to the pan. Once the butter has melted, add the marinated shrimp with the dressing and cook, tossing occasionally, until they are no longer translucent, 3 to 4 minutes. Remove the shrimp and set aside.

6 Add the remaining 2 tablespoons of butter to the pan. Once the butter has melted, add the linguine, about ½ cup of the reserved pasta liquid (more if needed), and the arugula. Toss until the arugula is wilted, about 2 minutes. Season with salt and pepper and the pecorino Romano. Add the sausage, shrimp, and nuts and cook until all elements are warm.

CACIO E PEPE

Kosher salt

1 pound dried spaghetti

4 tablespoons (½ stick) unsalted butter

3½ cups finely grated pecorino Romano cheese, plus more for serving

2 teaspoons crushed black peppercorns

Serves 4 On the surface, this is a simple salt-and-pepper pasta, but it's arguably one of the most famous dishes of Rome (although RPM Italian in Chicago, Illinois, serves a pretty outstanding rendition as well). If executed right, this very simple dish can be absolutely extraordinary.

1 Bring a large pot of heavily salted water to a boil over high heat.

2 Add the pasta and cook until slightly al dente (it should be a bit chewy). Reserve 1 cup of the cooking water, then drain the pasta in a colander.

3 Over low heat, melt the butter in the same pasta pot. Add the pasta and ½ cup of the reserved cooking water, and stir, adding more water if necessary. Add the cheese and pepper and stir until the cheese has melted and forms a creamy sauce, about 5 minutes. Serve with additional cheese.

SLOW COOKER LAMB RAGU LINGUINE
with CRISPY FRIED FIGS

2 tablespoons olive oil, divided

2 pounds lamb loin, cut into 1-inch cubes

1 6-ounce can of tomato paste

1 14-ounce can of San Marzano whole tomatoes

Cloves from 1 head of garlic, crushed

1 large onion, chopped

1 cup red wine

2 bay leaves

Kosher salt and freshly ground black pepper to taste

3 fresh figs, quartered

1 pound linguine

Serves 6 When I was growing up, Bushwick, Brooklyn, was a rough, raw place where few non-neighborhood people would venture if they had hopes of returning home again. Then Brooklyn became hip and cool, and Bushwick was relabeled—pause while I laugh—East Williamsburg. In this modern version of a once terrifying place, there is an amazing restaurant called Roberta's. While their pizzas have garnered them quite a bit of attention, it's their pastas I find extraordinary, and they provided the inspiration for this dish. Too often meat sauces like Bolognese can be heavy, tomato-laden versions of chili or sloppy joe filling. Here the lamb is infused with flavor through long, slow cooking so you don't need a ton of sauce to weigh down the pasta. This recipe calls for a slow cooker, which lets you put all your ingredients in it in the morning then return to something really delicious for dinner.

1 Remove the insert from your slow cooker (if your slow cooker doesn't have a removable insert, use a Dutch oven) and place it over high heat on your stove top. Add 1 tablespoon of the olive oil. Once the oil is hot, add the lamb and cook until browned, about 5 minutes. Return the insert to the slow cooker (or transfer the meat and oil from the Dutch oven to the slow cooker) and add the tomato paste, tomatoes, garlic, onion, red wine, bay leaves, salt, and pepper. Cook on high for 3 hours, or according to your slow cooker instructions.

2 In a medium skillet set over medium-high heat, heat the remaining 1 tablespoon of olive oil. Add the figs and fry until crispy.

RECIPE CONTINUES

3   Bring a large pot of heavily salted water to a boil over high heat. Add the pasta and cook until slightly al dente (it should be a bit chewy). Reserve 1 cup of the cooking water, then drain the pasta in a colander.

4   In a large pot set over medium heat, combine the pasta and ½ cup of the reserved pasta cooking water, and stir, adding more water if necessary. Stir in the figs and the lamb ragu until all the ingredients are fully incorporated. Serve hot.

SPICY CHICKEN AND SHRIMP PENNE
À LA VODKA

½ cup plus 2 tablespoons olive oil, divided

1 large onion, chopped

5 garlic cloves, chopped

1 teaspoon salt

5 baseball-size tomatoes, chopped

½ cup vodka

1 cup heavy cream

1 cup shredded mozzarella cheese

Kosher salt, for cooking the pasta

1 pound dried penne

1 teaspoon crushed red pepper flakes

2 skinless, boneless chicken breasts, sliced

1 pound medium shrimp, peeled and deveined

Serves 4 I was never a big à la vodka fan, but after trying a recipe from my cousin Blake and combining some dimensions from a sauce from one of my favorite pizzerias—Carmine's in Williamsburg, Brooklyn—I brought up a little bit of the spiciness in this recipe to cut through the richness of the à la vodka sauce. I happen to like the combination of chicken and shrimp, because of the different ways they respond to the sauce.

1 In a large pot set over high heat, heat ½ cup of the olive oil. Add the onion, garlic, salt, and tomatoes. Stir and cook until the tomatoes are reduced to a paste, about 20 minutes.

2 Pour in the vodka. Place a long matchstick or long-handled lighter over the pot to light the vodka (being very careful not to burn yourself). The fire will go out after the alcohol burns off, about 1 minute. Fold in the cream and mozzarella cheese. Reduce the heat to low to keep the sauce warm.

3 In a separate large pot, bring heavily salted water to a boil over high heat. Add the pasta and cook until slightly al dente (it should be a bit chewy). Reserve 1 cup of the cooking water, then drain the pasta in a colander.

4 In a large skillet set over high heat, heat the remaining 2 tablespoons of olive oil. Add the red pepper flakes. After about 30 seconds, add the chicken and cook, stirring occasionally, for about 3 minutes. Add the shrimp and cook until the chicken and shrimp are fully cooked, about 6 minutes.

5 Increase the heat under the vodka-cream-cheese sauce to medium and pour in ½ cup of the reserved pasta water. Stir in the pasta, shrimp, and chicken. Cook until all the ingredients are hot, adding more pasta water if too thick, and serve.

EASY CARBONARA

½ pound bacon, about 8 slices

1 tablespoon dried oregano

Kosher salt, for cooking the pasta

1 pound dried spaghetti

2 garlic cloves, minced

2 tablespoons olive oil

2 large eggs

1 cup freshly grated Parmesan cheese

Serves 4 This was a recipe I put together for a stage show I used to do at colleges. I wanted to emphasize how good ingredients don't have to be expensive and that you don't need expensive cookware to make great food. It's essentially the bacon and eggs of the pasta world! While Italians commonly use guanciale, or cured pork cheeks, in their carbonaras, I urge you to embrace the meat candy that is bacon. Timing and stirring are crucial here—and I urge you to use extreme care, as you are cooking with and consuming what are essentially raw eggs, or eggs just barely cooked, so only use high-quality fresh eggs. But when you put it all together, and combine all the ingredients just right, it's like velvet in your mouth.

1 Using a George Foreman grill, lay the bacon on the grill, season with the oregano, and cook until crispy. There will be a lot of oil that pools in the "fat catcher" and the space between the grills. Reserve this green oil and the cooked bacon. (Alternately, preheat an oven to 375°F. Place a metal rack over a baking sheet and lay the bacon on the rack. Season with the oregano. Place the baking sheet in the oven and cook the bacon for approximately 20 minutes. Turn the bacon and cook until crispy, about an additional 10 minutes. Remove the bacon from the oven, reserving the oil.)

2 Bring a large pot of heavily salted water to a boil over high heat. Add the pasta and cook until slightly al dente (it should be a bit chewy). Reserve 1 cup of the cooking water, then drain the pasta in a colander.

3 In a large bowl, combine the hot pasta, ½ cup of the reserved water, the reserved green oil, and the bacon, garlic, and olive oil, and stir, adding more water if necessary. Crack the eggs into the bowl and add the cheese. Stir rigorously to thoroughly combine all the ingredients. Serve immediately.

SPAGHETTI PIE

1 pound spaghetti, cooked (leftover is fine)

3 large eggs

1 cup grated Parmesan cheese

1½ cups shredded mozzarella, divided

1 cup tomato paste, divided

2 tablespoons olive oil

Serves 4 I was first introduced to a variation of this recipe by a fraternity brother from Emory University named Matt Sacks. Later on, while in graduate school, my stepmother—a pretty great cook in her own right—gave me her version of the recipe, which comes in handy not only as a great lunch or dinner, but also as leftovers that I can make and eat throughout the week. It operates on the same principle as a baked ziti, so feel free to change up the type of pasta or type of cheese or sauce as you see fit. But give the old classics a try—they are classics for a reason, after all!

1 Preheat the oven to 350°F.

2 In a large bowl, mix together the pasta, eggs, Parmesan cheese, 1 cup of the mozzarella, and ¾ cup of the tomato paste.

3 Grease a pie tin (or Pyrex pie plate) with the olive oil. Add the remaining ¼ cup of tomato paste to the pie tin and press the pasta into it. Top with the remaining ½ cup of mozzarella.

4 Bake the pie in the oven for 30 to 35 minutes. Remove the pie from the oven and use a pizza slicer to cut it into wedges. Serve with a green salad.

SIDES & SALADS

CHEF SANG YOON OF FATHER'S OFFICE IN SANTA MONICA, California, home to what is arguably one of the finest burgers mankind has created, has his own November holiday tradition when it comes to dining. It is called Sangsgiving. He rejects turkey, which he considers boring, dry, and overdone. As he says, "When you think of Thanksgiving, it's not the turkey you think of but rather the side dishes: the mashed potatoes, stuffing, and so on." Though he is certainly off base when it comes to *my* personal turkey, of course he is right about the allure of great side dishes. I'm sure I'm not the only one who has gone to a restaurant and requested a selection of sides in lieu of an entrée. In many meals, a great side can even steal the spotlight from the main attraction. The super-stellar sides you'll find in this chapter are sure to punch up your plate or please all on their own.

And salad? Once a dirty word in most meat-and-potato cultures, salad is no longer served as a mere prequel, a coming attraction to the "real" food. It can be a main dish on its own with every bit as savory and nuanced an amalgam of flavors and textures. In these recipes, contrasts of tastes, temperatures, and ingredients propel the simple salad to a place that's anything but simple—a place that is straight up tasty.

CAULIFLOWER BRANDADE

4 cups beef stock

1 head of cauliflower, stem and leaves discarded, and cut into bite-size florets

½ cup olive oil

6 garlic cloves, chopped

1 2.8-ounce jar of Italian salt-packed anchovies

Kosher salt and freshly ground black pepper to taste

½ pound Chimay cheese (or your favorite semi-soft cheese)

Serves 4 I developed this sumptuous side dish completely by accident. It began as a recipe my mother was given by a colleague. While attempting it, I overcooked the cauliflower, so much so that when I went to sauté it with the anchovies, garlic, and oil, it broke down into a mash. Having recently had a similar dish at a friend's restaurant, I decided to go with it and play up the velvety consistency by adding some Chimay cheese. Why did I use that type of cheese? Honestly, I had some left over from a cheese platter, but, happily, it was just the right touch.

1 In a large pot set over high heat, bring the beef stock to a boil. Add the cauliflower. If the stock doesn't cover the cauliflower, add water until the florets are just covered. Bring back to a boil and then reduce the heat to a simmer. Cook until the florets are fork-tender, approximately 10 to 12 minutes.

2 Preheat the broiler.

3 Place a large ovenproof skillet over medium-high heat. Once the pan is hot, add the oil, garlic, and anchovies. Cook, stirring occasionally, until the garlic is golden brown, about 3 minutes. Remove the pan from the heat and add the cauliflower and its stock, stirring with a wooden spoon. Season with salt and pepper.

4 Tear the cheese into small pieces and fold them into the cauliflower mixture. Transfer the pan to the oven for 1 to 2 minutes, just to brown the top a little. Serve with toast points, crudités, or as an accompaniment to grilled meat or fish.

EDAMAME-ROASTED CORN SUCCOTASH

4 ears corn

Kosher salt to taste

2 cups frozen, shelled edamame

4 tablespoons (½ stick) unsalted butter

1 large white onion, finely diced

⅓ cup finely chopped chives

Serves 6 to 8 The summer before I left for graduate school, I worked at the Greenmarket in Lower Manhattan's Union Square. It was amazing. I got paid in cash, they paid for my lunch, and I was able to use fruit I did not own to barter for fresh vegetables from all around the state. This was also the year I began cooking seriously and studying culinary craft. The inspiration for this dish comes from my friend Lincoln Williams, who was at the time working at a restaurant called Alouette. I would often bring home the veggies I had gotten, and he would have some fun little bits he had gotten from work or at the fish market. Since I was dating his roommate at the time, we would create some kind of culinary mash-up together. The focus, however, was always the fresh veggies—especially roasted summer corn. This recipe makes a great side dish at any barbecue.

1 Preheat the oven to 350°F.

2 Remove the silk and outer husks from the corn, but keep the inner layers intact. Run each ear under water. Microwave the corn on high for 5 to 6 minutes, until softened.

3 Transfer the corn to a baking sheet and roast it in the oven for another 5 minutes, or until the corn is fully cooked. Cool, then slice the kernels off the cob.

4 In a medium saucepan, bring 2 inches of salted water to a boil. Add the edamame and simmer until soft, approximately 5 minutes. Drain the edamame.

5 In a large skillet set over high heat, melt the butter. Add the onion and cook until softened, 3 to 4 minutes. Add the edamame and corn; season with salt and cook for about 1 minute, stirring. Remove the pan from the heat and stir in the chives. Serve warm.

GRILLED ASPARAGUS RAFTS

2 bunches of thick asparagus
spears (about 24)

4 wooden skewers

¼ cup olive oil

Flaky sea salt to taste

Freshly cracked black pepper
to taste

Serves 6 When you read this you may think, *That's a recipe?* Yes, it is! Skewering the asparagus spears together into a "raft" makes them easier to flip and easier to cook evenly. Trust me, you'll thank me once you've tried this. Be sure to use great-quality olive oil and great-quality salt—you will have an exponentially better final product.

1 Preheat the oven to 350°F.

2 Snap off the ends of the asparagus where they break, then trim all the stalks to the same length. Line half the spears up side by side, and thread 2 skewers through the aligned spears to hold them all together like a raft. Repeat with the remaining spears and skewers.

3 Place the "rafts" on a rimmed baking sheet. Drizzle the rafts with the olive oil and season with salt and pepper.

4 Place the baking sheet in the oven and roast the rafts for 10 minutes. Turn the rafts over and roast for another 10 minutes, or until tender but still crunchy. Pile the rafts onto a warmed platter and let your guests slide a few spears onto their plates.

CRAB CAKE DRESSING

2 tablespoons unsalted butter

20 slices of white bread, cubed

1 pound lump crabmeat, picked over for shells and cartilage

1 large onion, finely chopped

2 celery stalks, finely chopped

5 large eggs, lightly beaten

Kosher salt and freshly ground black pepper to taste

2 tablespoons chopped fresh cilantro

2 cups chicken broth, or more as needed

2 tablespoons freshly squeezed lemon juice

Serves 12 to 14 Okay, let's be honest: crab cakes are freakin' amazing. You know it, I know it, the entire state of Maryland knows it. DC knows it (but if they told you, they would have to kill you). After trying several crab cakes in Baltimore and the surrounding counties, I realized that despite the fact that the cakes were prepared with incredibly light crabmeat, they have a wonderful heartiness. This made me wonder how crab cakes would function in a Thanksgiving dressing. So, in essence, this recipe is a tray full of crab cakes, with the bread and vegetable aspects turned up to provide a great counterpoint to the flavors we usually expect for Thanksgiving. It has the lightness of crab cakes, with the hearty, gravy absorbability of good Thanksgiving dressing—my homage to surf and turf.

1 Preheat the oven to 325°F. Grease a 9 × 13-inch baking dish with the butter.

2 In a large bowl, mix all the remaining ingredients together until well combined. (Add more broth if the mixture doesn't hold together.)

3 Turn the mixture into the baking dish. Bake for 1 hour, or until the top is brown and crisp.

MOM'S SPINACH PIE

1½ tablespoons olive oil

1 large onion, diced

Kosher salt and freshly ground black pepper to taste

3 10-ounce boxes of frozen chopped spinach, defrosted

1 pound low-fat ricotta cheese

1 pound part-skim mozzarella cheese, cut into small chunks or shredded

2 large eggs, beaten

¾ cup dry bread crumbs (I favor Progresso Italian bread crumbs for mine)

2 teaspoons garlic powder

½ cup grated cheese (Parmesan or Locatelli), for topping (optional)

Serves 8 I often spike my spinach pie with a little garlic powder, but that's about the only refinement I've made to this crustless pie, one of my mom's classic dishes. When my mom would ask if there were any "requests" foodwise when I'd come home from college, this was always at the top of my list. It may be served as a vegetarian main dish, accompanied by a simple baked potato and salad, or as a side dish. Heck, you can cut a slice from the leftovers and serve it inside an omelet! Adjust the amount and types of cheese to your taste, and the "pie" can also be prepared in a pastry or phyllo dough crust if you prefer, though, personally, I don't think it needs it. You could make this recipe with fresh spinach, but I've had great, consistent results with frozen spinach; it's an ultra-convenient product and you can't beat the price.

1 Preheat the oven to 350°F. Grease a large glass or ceramic baking dish with about ½ tablespoon of olive oil.

2 In a medium saucepan set over medium-low heat, heat the remaining 1 tablespoon of olive oil. Add the diced onion and a large pinch of salt. Sauté until the onion is translucent, about 3 minutes. Remove the pan from the heat and transfer the onions to a large bowl.

3 Add the spinach, ricotta, ¾ of the mozzarella, eggs, bread crumbs, garlic powder, salt, and pepper to the bowl and stir to combine. Scrape the mixture into the prepared baking dish and top with the remaining mozzarella. Sprinkle with the grated cheese, if using.

4 Bake for 45 minutes, until the pie is set and the top is golden and slightly crusty.

5 To serve, cut into wedges or just spoon onto plates.

SMOKED PAPRIKA ONION RINGS

3 Vidalia onions (or other sweet onion), peeled

2 cups all-purpose flour

2 large eggs, beaten

2 cups panko bread crumbs

3 tablespoons sweet smoked paprika

Vegetable or peanut oil, for deep frying

Kosher salt to taste

Serves a crowd When I serve up flavorful burgers and artisanal sausages, two of my go-tos for entertaining, I need side dishes that will stand up to the bold flavors of the entrée. The addition of smoked paprika works extremely well with the onion rings and makes them a standout dish. My favorite onions to use for these are sweet Georgia Vidalia onions, but Maui or Walla Walla onions would be great, too. They don't need a dipping sauce, but a little bit of ranch dressing wouldn't hurt nobody.

1 Using a mandolin or a very sharp knife, slice the onions into ¼-inch-thick rounds. Separate the rounds into rings.

2 Place the flour, beaten eggs, and panko in three separate shallow bowls. Mix a tablespoon of paprika into each bowl.

3 Dredge the onion rings first in the flour, then in the eggs, and finally in the panko. Place the dredged rings on a baking sheet and allow the coating to set for 10 minutes.

4 In a large pot set over medium-high heat, bring about 4 inches of oil to 365°F (use a deep-frying or candy thermometer to check the temperature).

5 Line a separate baking sheet with paper towels. Working in batches, fry the onion rings until golden brown, 2 to 3 minutes per side. When done, the rings should float to the surface of the oil. Transfer each batch of fried rings to the prepared baking sheet and season with salt.

6 Keep the finished onion rings warm under layers of paper towels as you cook the remaining batches. Serve hot.

MISO-ROASTED VEGGIES

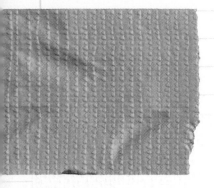

Serves 6 to 8 In this recipe, miso brings out the richness of the vegetables. Depending upon the combination of vegetables you use, you may find one type of miso paste more appropriate than another, so let your taste buds be your guide. I dust the vegetables very, very liberally with garlic powder—almost like a heavy snowfall of the stuff—which really makes the dish. This makes an incredible side dish for the fall, thanks to its autumnal colors and tremendous heartiness, and it delivers a boatload of great phytonutrients from the veggies!

¼ cup olive oil

½ cup miso paste (yellow or mild works well with the vegetables here)

3 sweet potatoes, peeled and cubed

3 beets, peeled and cubed

2 12-ounce bags of broccoli florets

2 Spanish onions, cubed

1 head of garlic, separated into cloves and peeled

¼ cup garlic powder (not granulated garlic) or more to taste

1 Preheat the oven to 375°F.

2 In a large bowl, combine the oil and the miso. Add the sweet potatoes, beets, broccoli, onions, and garlic cloves and toss to coat.

3 Spray a 9 × 13-inch baking pan with nonstick cooking spray and add about ¼ inch of water. Add the vegetables to the pan. Dust everything with the garlic powder. Cover the whole dish with aluminum foil.

4 Roast the vegetables for 50 minutes. Remove the foil, stir the veggies, and cook uncovered for an additional 10 minutes, or until the sweet potatoes and beets are fully cooked. Serve hot or warm.

SPAGHETTI-STYLE SPAGHETTI SQUASH

1 large spaghetti squash

1 tablespoon extra-virgin olive oil

2 Italian pork (or veggie) sausages

1 16-ounce can of San Marzano crushed tomatoes

1 cup fresh ricotta

Sea salt to taste

¼ cup fresh basil leaves, cut into chiffonade

½ cup grated Parmesan

Serves 4 to 6 We live in an age of relentless pursuit of physical perfection and betterment. Nobody likes man boobs! Nobody likes having triceps wings! There is nothing that people love about their love handles! So people are cutting out carbs. Left, right, and center—bread is increasingly dead. But there are alternatives that don't suck. Spaghetti squash can be used and treated like noodles . . . and while in no way does it re-create the exact texture or consistency of pasta, you can still make a very rich and satisfying dish without the calories of traditional spaghetti. The classic Italian combination of tomatoes and ricotta has a tangy creaminess that makes this less like a slaw and more like a real pasta dish.

1 Using a sturdy fork, take out all of your aggression on the spaghetti squash, stabbing into the flesh Norman Bates–style until it has a bunch of holes in it.

2 Place the squash in the microwave and cook on high for about 12 minutes, or until it is tender when pierced with a fork.

3 In a large sauté pan set over high heat, heat the olive oil and cook the sausages until brown on all sides, 4 to 5 minutes. Transfer the sausages to a cutting board, reserving the cooking liquid in the pan, and cut them into ½-inch-long pieces.

4 Add the tomatoes and their juices to the pan the sausages cooked in and simmer for 5 minutes. Remove from the heat and stir in the ricotta.

5 Slice the squash in half and remove the seeds, then use a fork to scrape the "spaghetti" strands from the squash into a large bowl. Pour in the sausage cooking liquid, the crushed tomatoes, and the ricotta. Stir together with a wooden spoon until well combined. Season with salt. Fold in the chopped sausage, basil, and Parmesan. Serve warm.

ELOTE (CORN ON THE COB)

½ cup unsalted butter (1 stick), softened

⅓ cup chopped fresh cilantro

4 garlic cloves, minced

4 ears corn, shucked and silk removed, but with a partial stalk kept on as a handle

½ cup Japanese Kewpie mayonnaise (or your favorite mayonnaise)

½ cup grated Cotija cheese

4 teaspoons paprika

1 lime, cut into 4 wedges

Serves 4   This is, without question, my favorite Mexican street food. It's kind of amazing how adding just a few elements to the corn creates a sensation that is so balanced and yet hits your palate on every level: sour from the lime, creamy from the Cotija cheese and mayo, and a little bit of a bite from the garlic, with the savory perfume of paprika setting off the sweet corn itself. Feel free to experiment and add embellishments like toasted pumpkin seeds or sesame seeds.

1 In a small bowl, mix the butter with the cilantro and garlic until well combined.

2 Preheat a grill or a ridged grill pan over medium-high heat.

3 Grill the corn until hot and lightly charred all over, 7 to 10 minutes.

4 Coat the ears in the seasoned butter. Wrap each ear in aluminum foil and place the corn on the grill for another 2 minutes.

5 Unwrap the ears and spread them evenly with the mayonnaise. Sprinkle with Cotija cheese, dust with paprika, and serve hot with a lime wedge to squeeze over the top.

WILD MUSHROOM TART

4 tablespoons extra-virgin olive oil, plus more for greasing the baking sheet

½ pound (8 sheets) frozen phyllo dough, thawed

½ cup panko bread crumbs

1 large egg, lightly beaten, for the egg wash

5 tablespoons unsalted butter

1 large leek, sliced in half lengthwise, washed, and finely chopped

Sea salt and freshly ground black pepper to taste

4 cups assorted sliced mushrooms (shiitake, enoki, mitsutake, button, morels, whatever's in season)

5 garlic cloves, smashed

¾ cup fruity red wine, such as Merlot

¾ cup beef stock (optional; if not using, double the red wine)

¾ cup fresh ricotta

½ cup grated Parmigiano-Reggiano

1 tablespoon garlic powder

¼ cup grated Fontina cheese

Serves 6 to 8 or more as a canapé A winter go-to in my house, this tart uses phyllo to create what is basically a light, pastry-like pizza crust. Feel free to experiment with many different varieties of mushrooms, but always use great olive oil with the panko crumbs between the layers of pastry. I make sure that the mushrooms and leeks are cooked down to the point of softness—nothing ruins this more than taking a bite and having to fight through a mealy mushroom or an uncooked leek. This tart can be cut into strips and served alongside a salad or served as a snack with cocktails as you would bruschetta.

1   Lightly grease a rimmed baking sheet with olive oil. Lay a sheet of phyllo down on the oiled baking sheet. Brush with oil, leaving a 2-inch unoiled border around the whole sheet. Dust with a scant tablespoon of panko on top of the oil. Lay another phyllo sheet down and repeat, continuing until you have used all the phyllo.

2   Brush the beaten egg wash along the entire un-oiled border. Roll the border about 1 inch toward the center to create a raised edge. Brush the border with the egg wash. Set the phyllo crust aside.

3   In a large sauté pan set over medium heat, melt 3 tablespoons of the butter. Add the leek and cook, stirring occasionally, until softened, about 5 minutes. Season with sea salt and pepper, and drizzle with a little olive oil. Remove the leek, but reserve the oil in the pan.

4   Get the pan hot again, then add the mushrooms, adding the firmer ones first. Cook until softened, about 9 minutes. Season with more salt and pepper. Add the garlic and cook to lightly brown. Stir in the wine, the remaining 2 tablespoons of butter, and the beef stock (if using). Cook until the mushrooms are very soft and have absorbed most of the liquid, about 12 minutes. Stir the leeks back into the mixture and remove the pan from the heat.

5 Preheat the oven to 350°F.

6 In a small bowl, combine the ricotta, Parmigiano-Reggiano, and garlic powder into a thick paste.

7 Spread the ricotta paste on top of the phyllo crust inside the rolled edge. Top with the mushroom-leek mixture. Cover with aluminum foil and bake for 15 minutes. Uncover, top with the Fontina, and bake for another 10 to 12 minutes, or until the pie is crispy and browned. Cut into squares and serve hot.

ROASTED MUSHROOMS IN A POUCH

Serves 3 to 4

This may just be the simplest and best way there is to cook mushrooms. Use the most exotic mushrooms you can get your hands on.

1 pound mixed mushrooms, washed and trimmed, halved or quartered if large

¼ cup extra-virgin olive oil

2½ tablespoons sea salt

1 Preheat the oven to 350°F.

2 Pile the mushrooms in the center of a large sheet of heavy-duty aluminum foil, and toss with olive oil and sea salt. Bring the long edges of the aluminum foil together and fold over three times to seal. Crimp the short ends of the foil together to make a pouch.

3 Place the pouch on the top rack of the oven, and roast for 25 minutes. Carefully rip open the pouch and spill the mushrooms into a serving dish.

TWICE-BAKED SWEET POTATOES

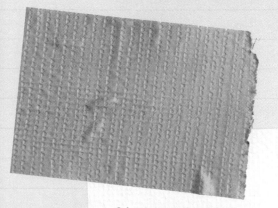

6 large sweet potatoes

Olive oil, for roasting

2 cups ricotta cheese

⅓ cup bourbon (optional)

6 tablespoons unsalted butter, melted

1 bunch of fresh chives, finely chopped

1½ cups grated Fontina cheese

Serves 6 Mom used to make twice-baked potatoes for company, and I was always envious of her guests. I decided to put my own stamp on the recipe and at the same time create a delicious showcase for Red Stag Honey Tea, an amazingly fun flavored bourbon from Jim Beam out of the Bluegrass State of Kentucky. The bourbon adds a sweetness that plays nicely off the punch of the big, salty flavors provided by the Fontina and chives. And it is a well-known fact that bourbon is to butter as Butch was to Sundance.

1 Preheat the oven to 400°F. Line a rimmed baking sheet with aluminum foil.

2 Using a fork, poke holes in the sweet potatoes. Rub the skins with olive oil and place the potatoes on the prepared baking sheet. Bake until a fork can slide easily into a potato, 1 to 1½ hours. Remove the potatoes from the oven and let cool completely. Keep the oven on at 400°F.

3 Slice off the top third of each potato lengthwise and discard. Scoop most of the flesh of the potatoes into a large bowl, leaving just fairly thin shells, thereby turning the skins into potato canoes.

4 Add the ricotta to the cooled potato flesh and combine well. Stir in the bourbon, if using, and the melted butter, then add half of the chopped chives. Spoon the mixture back into the potato canoes and arrange the potatoes on a rimmed baking sheet.

5 Bake the potatoes for 15 minutes, then remove them from the oven and top with the Fontina cheese. Return the potatoes to the oven and bake until the Fontina is melted and the potatoes are golden, another 5 to 7 minutes. Top the potatoes with the remaining chopped chives and serve hot.

CREAMIEST DAMN MASHED POTATOES EVER

4 to 6 large Yukon Gold
  potatoes, peeled

2 tablespoons extra-virgin
  olive oil

½ cup whole milk

½ cup heavy cream

¼ pound high-fat unsalted
  butter, such as Kerrygold,
  cubed

1 cup mascarpone cheese

Kosher salt to taste

Serves 6 to 8 Ordinary mashed potatoes are easy: you peel potatoes, boil them, and mash them. But how do you make them amazing? This mascarpone-enriched version is a good place to start. While there are many schools of thought on mashed potatoes, I have seldom made fluffier mashed potatoes than I have when using an immersion or stick blender. It is a reasonably priced piece of kitchen equipment that will yield many culinary dividends over time—it's great for mixing sauces, incorporating ingredients, and, yes, making the fluffiest damn mashed potatoes ever. Lately, I sometimes add burrata or ricotta to the mash, but mascarpone will always be my go-to; it's sweet, creamy, and fluffy—like me. And while I offer black pepper at the table for those who want it, I don't use it to season the potatoes, as I think it takes away from the buttery flavor. These potatoes are a great addition to sandwiches and keep very well in the fridge.

1 Put the potatoes in a large pot with water to cover by 1 inch. Bring to a boil over high heat and then reduce the heat to a simmer. Cook until the potatoes are very soft, about 30 minutes.

2 Drain the potatoes in a colander and return them to the empty pot. Drizzle with the olive oil, then pour in the milk and cream. Using an immersion blender, combine all the ingredients until the potatoes are mostly smooth. Add the butter a few pieces at a time, blending continuously. Be sure to lift and fold with the immersion blender; you want to get as much air as you can into the potatoes, not create a gummy paste.

3 Make a well in the center of the potatoes and add the mascarpone. Blend again until the cheese is fully incorporated. Season with salt and serve hot.

WARM SPINACH SALAD
WITH GOCHUJANG BACON

½ pound bacon

¼ cup sesame oil

1 cup gochujang

2 tablespoons raw sesame seeds

4 to 5 tablespoons unsalted butter, divided

2 bunches of spinach, washed and stemmed

1 cup chopped walnuts

1 pound cylindrical rice cake (dduk), cut into ½-inch pieces (optional)

4 large eggs

Serves 4 Gochujang, a spicy chili paste made from fermented rice and soybeans, is a Korean staple that does amazing things for the flavor of pork and beef. I consider it one of the most underused seasonings around. Coating the bacon with gochujang before baking it adds lots of flavor and gives the fermented bean paste a chance to cook into the meat. Starchy, crispy dduk serves as a stand-in for croutons, bringing East to West in a delicious and fun way. Both gochujang and dduk, a glutinous rice product that comes in long, slender cylinders, can be found at Korean markets or ordered online.

1 Prepare the bacon: Cut the strips of bacon in half. In a small plastic container, mix the sliced bacon with the sesame oil and gochujang, turning the strips to coat them completely. Cover and refrigerate for 3 hours or overnight.

2 Preheat the oven to 400°F. Line a rimmed baking sheet with aluminum foil.

3 Arrange the seasoned bacon on the prepared baking sheet and sprinkle with the sesame seeds. Bake for 15 minutes, turning the slices after 8 minutes. Remove from the oven and let cool.

4 In a large skillet set over medium heat, melt 2 tablespoons of the butter. Add the spinach leaves and stir to coat. Cook just until the spinach is wilted, and immediately divide the mixture among 4 serving bowls. Top with the walnuts.

5 If using the dduk rice cakes: Melt 1 tablespoon of the butter in a skillet over high heat. Add the rice cakes and fry until crispy. Place a rice cake on top of the spinach in each bowl.

6 Add the 2 remaining tablespoons of butter to the skillet. Crack the eggs into the pan and cook them sunny side up. Place an egg on top of each serving.

7 Arrange the bacon pieces over the eggs and serve immediately.

SIMPLE KOREAN GREEN ONION SESAME SALAD

3 bunches of green onions (thick bulbs are easier to shave)

3 teaspoons rice wine vinegar

¼ cup sesame oil

2 tablespoons sesame seeds

Serves 4 I first had this dish as part of a *banchan* (an array of small dishes that accompany a Korean meal) at Miss Korea BBQ on West Thirty-Second Street in New York City. I love green onions, and served at the height of freshness, tossed with sesame oil, and a little bit of vinegar, they make a wonderful palate cleanser and a great delicious, crunchy salad dish.

1 Trim the roots and wilted ends from the green onions. Use a vegetable peeler to shave the bulbs into long strips. Rinse the onions in cold water.

2 Just before serving, stir together the vinegar, sesame oil, and sesame seeds in a large bowl. Add the shredded green onions and toss to coat.

SAUCES & CONDIMENTS

**If kids can learn how to make a simple
Bolognese sauce, they will never go hungry.
It's pretty easy to cook pasta, but a good
sauce is way more useful.**
—Emeril Lagasse

**When facing a difficult task, act as though it is
impossible to fail. If you are going after Moby Dick,
take along the tartar sauce.**
—H. Jackson Brown Jr.

VARIETY ISN'T THE SPICE OF LIFE—*SPICE* IS!

Yes, I am all for purity of ingredients; yes, I, too, have seen a chef, as
Anthony Bourdain says, "die a little inside" when a diner douses a dish
they have prepared so carefully with sauce. But a great sauce can also
turn leftovers into magic, mundane ingredients into gourmet morsels,
and plain pasta or rice into a memorable meal. These sauces are a
few that I like to have in my arsenal, so to speak, when the moment of
flavorlessness happens to arise. They ensure that my French fries will
never go naked, will always have the dopest dippin' sauces, and will
forever be the straight up tastiest!

EASY-ASS SALSA

3 ripe tomatoes

1 jalapeño, seeded and diced

¼ cup chopped fresh cilantro

Juice of 1 lime

1 garlic clove, minced

Kosher salt

Makes 2½ cups If you have good tomatoes, nothing could be simpler or better than a fresh salsa to dollop onto tacos, serve with grilled meat and fish, or just scoop up with chips.

1 Dice the tomatoes, and place them in a medium bowl, saving as much of the juices as possible.

2 Add the jalapeño, cilantro, lime juice, and garlic, and season with salt to taste. Cover and refrigerate for at least 1 hour.

PICKLED RED ONIONS

¾ cup rice wine vinegar or white vinegar

½ teaspoon sugar

½ teaspoon salt

1 medium red onion, sliced

Makes about 1 cup These onions will keep for up to 2 weeks in the refrigerator. You'll be glad you have them, trust me. They do wonders for so many dishes.

1 In a jar or container with a tight-fitting lid, combine the vinegar, sugar, and salt. Stir to dissolve.

2 Bring about 3 cups of water to a boil. Place the onion in a colander in the sink. Pour the boiling water over the onion and shake to drain.

3 Add the onion to the pickling brine and stir. Cover with the lid and place the container in the refrigerator. The onion will be ready in about 2 hours. Store in the refrigerator for up to 2 weeks.

CANDIED BOURBON BACON

1 pound thick-sliced bacon
¼ cup bourbon
½ cup (packed) brown sugar
Canola oil for baking sheet

Makes 1 pound These things are so addictive, my friend has described them as dog treats for adults. Keep the bacon in a sealed container, with wax paper separating the layers.

1 Separate the bacon strips and place them in a sealable plastic bag. Add the bourbon, seal, and refrigerate overnight.

2 Preheat the oven to 350°F.

3 Pat the bacon dry, discarding the marinade. Put in a large bowl and thoroughly coat it with half the brown sugar.

4 Lay the bacon strips flat on a lightly oiled rimmed baking sheet. Dust with the remaining brown sugar, and bake until shiny and caramel brown, about 20 minutes. Let cool.

5 Store the candied bacon in the refrigerator for up to 4 days. Chop it into small bits before serving.

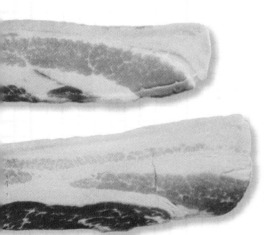

LET'S TALK ABOUT BOURBON

Bourbon is America's whiskey, hailing from the great state of Kentucky. In bourbon the flavors of corn, bluegrass, and limestone coalesce into pure magic that has been celebrated by everyone from Derby ladies in their giant hats to cardigan-wearing hipsters in Brooklyn, Portland, and all points in between.

Bourbon is warm, honey-like, toasty, and sweet and needs to be part of your repertoire before you drink one more appletini. I'm dead serious. Try it, or we can't be friends.

While much is made of Pappy Van Winkle, and I have sampled every aged variation I can get my hands on, it still doesn't do it for me. My favorites are, in no particular order: Bulleit, Four Roses, Basil Hayden, Angel's Envy, Michter's, Hudson Baby Bourbon, Woodford Reserve, Jim Beam Devil's Cut, Makers 46, Blanton's, and Buffalo Trace.

If you're gonna do it neat (no mixer) go with rocks (ice) and maybe a water or ginger back (a saloon-y euphemism for chaser); otherwise, if you insist on a mixer, ginger ale or ginger beer is a great choice, as is any citrus juice.

I've recently become enamored of the old-fashioned, the best of which I had at New York's PDT, where brilliant young mixologist Jeff Bell stirs up a stellar version with "bacon-washed" bourbon (yes, that's a thing) and orange zest.

SPICY MEAT SAUCE

1 tablespoon olive oil

¾ pound ground beef

6 garlic cloves, crushed

1 onion, diced

¼ teaspoon crushed red pepper flakes

Kosher salt and freshly ground black pepper to taste

1 28-ounce can of crushed tomatoes, preferably San Marzano

½ cup grated Parmesan

2 cups In upstate New York, in the Rochester area especially, there is a beloved condiment called "Meat Hot Sauce," a spicy, oily slurry of ground meat the consistency of watery applesauce. It's really not my thing. At all.

Granted, I didn't grow up with it. I did, however, grow up with access to unreal Italian food and great groceries. Unlike Rochester's version, my spicy meat sauce is hearty and rich and has enough heat to cut through that richness. It's awesome on pasta, over rice, on fries, nachos, or hot dogs. It can be used in an omelet, a scramble, or a casserole. It's heat, it's meat, get used to it.

1 In a large skillet set over medium-high heat, heat the oil. Add the beef and cook, breaking it up with a spoon, until browned, 4 to 5 minutes. Use a slotted spoon to transfer the meat to a paper towel–lined plate, reserving the fat in the pan.

2 Add the garlic and onion to the skillet. Once the onion is translucent, 5 to 6 minutes, stir in the red pepper flakes, salt, and pepper.

3 Add the tomatoes and bring to a simmer. Stir occasionally until slightly thickened, 8 to 10 minutes.

4 Stir in the Parmesan and remove the pan from the heat. Return the meat to the skillet and stir to combine. Serve or transfer to airtight storage containers and refrigerate for up to 3 days or freeze for up to 1 month.

BBQ SAUCE

2 6-ounce cans of tomato paste

⅔ cup white vinegar

¼ cup (packed) dark brown sugar

2 tablespoons onion powder

2 tablespoons garlic powder

2 tablespoons paprika

2 tablespoons honey

2 tablespoons kosher salt

2 tablespoons freshly ground black pepper

Makes 3 cups **Better than store-bought, trust me.**

1 In a medium saucepan, combine all the ingredients and stir to blend thoroughly. Place the pan over medium heat and stir continuously until the sauce is heated through. Do not allow it to come to a boil.

2 Remove the pan from the heat. The sauce can be used immediately, or, if reserving for a later use, allow it to cool, then refrigerate it in a tightly sealed container. It will keep for up to 2 weeks.

DRY RUB

½ cup (packed) dark brown sugar

2 tablespoons garlic powder

2 tablespoons onion powder

1½ tablespoons finely ground espresso

1 tablespoon chili powder

1 tablespoon sweet smoked paprika

1 tablespoon ground cumin

1 teaspoon cayenne pepper

1 tablespoon ground mustard powder

1½ teaspoons ground cinnamon

5 teaspoons kosher salt

1 tablespoon freshly ground black pepper

Makes 1 cup **Although this recipe makes a big batch, don't be tempted to cut it down; the rub will keep for several months. It's great have on hand to season burgers or a pork loin. I even use it to season cubes of meat before browning them for a stew.**

Place all the ingredients in a large bowl and stir to combine. Store in an airtight container in the pantry.

MORNAY SAUCE

Makes 1 quart A basic white sauce that comes in handy for all sorts of uses, including the Kentucky Hot Brown Bluegrass Sandwich on page 53.

½ cup (1 stick) unsalted butter

6 tablespoons all-purpose flour

4 cups whole milk

1 cup grated Gruyère cheese

Kosher salt and white pepper to taste

¼ teaspoon freshly grated nutmeg

1 In a saucepan set over medium-high heat, melt the butter. Slowly whisk in the flour. Whisk constantly until the mixture is pale yellow and frothy, about 1 minute. Do not allow the mixture to brown; reduce the heat if necessary. Whisk in the milk all at once and continue to cook and whisk until the sauce thickens and comes to a boil, 2 to 3 minutes.

2 Reduce the heat to low. Simmer for another 3 minutes.

3 Remove the pan from the heat, stir in the cheese, and season with salt, pepper, and the nutmeg, whisking until incorporated. If the sauce seems too thick, thin it with a little warm milk. Serve warm.

ROASTED GARLIC MAYO

1 head of garlic

1 tablespoon olive oil

½ cup Hellmann's Light
Mayonnaise

Makes ½ cup You may have noticed that I am partial to Hellmann's Light Mayonnaise, which I appreciate not only for its reduced caloric content but for its fresher (to my palate) taste. Stirring in roasted garlic makes a good thing better and incredibly versatile.

1 Preheat the oven to 400°F.

2 Peel off and discard the outer layers of the garlic skin, leaving the individual cloves intact. Using a knife, cut off about ½ inch of the top of the garlic head to expose the individual cloves.

3 Put the garlic in an oven-safe pan and rub the olive oil over the exposed cloves. Roast the garlic for 30 minutes, until the entire head is very soft.

4 Remove the pan from the oven and let the garlic cool. Squeeze the garlic cloves from their skins into a small bowl. Add the mayonnaise and whisk to blend thoroughly. Refrigerate in an airtight container.

WASABI MAYO

½ cup Hellmann's Light
Mayonnaise

2½ teaspoons wasabi paste

Makes about ½ cup Adding a bit of water to the wasabi paste to loosen it makes it easier to blend into the mayonnaise.

In a small bowl, whisk together the mayo and wasabi until well blended. Refrigerate in an airtight container until ready to use.

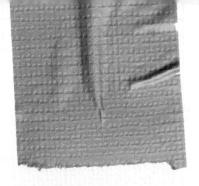

EASY KIMCHEE

1 large head of napa cabbage

2 tablespoons kosher salt

2 tablespoons rice wine vinegar

2 tablespoons gochujang

1 tablespoon fish sauce (optional)

1 tablespoon minced garlic

1 tablespoon peeled and minced fresh ginger

4 green onions, light-green and white parts only, sliced on the bias

Makes about 3 cups Perhaps the most ubiquitous food in all of Korea—as well as Koreatowns on both the East and West Coasts—is this spicy, fermented, crunchy cabbage wonderfulness known as kimchee. It serves as a pungent, acidic counterpoint to the richness of grilled beef and pork in the Korean barbecue tradition. Random fact: Our allies in the Korean War asked that the US government provide their soldiers with kimchee for its incredible health benefits. Traditionally, it is prepared in earthenware jars buried in the ground, with the contents left to ferment over time. This simplified recipe lets you re-create this awesome condiment without going the traditional route.

1 Remove and discard any wilted outer leaves from the cabbage, then halve it lengthwise. Chop the cabbage into wide ribbons.

2 In a large bowl, combine the cabbage with the salt. Set aside for 1 hour. Transfer the cabbage to a colander and rinse thoroughly to remove the excess salt. Let the cabbage stand in the colander for 30 minutes, or until it is dry and wilted.

3 Clean and dry the bowl. Add the vinegar, gochujang, fish sauce (if using), garlic, and ginger and mix together. Stir in the cabbage and green onions and combine thoroughly.

4 Transfer the cabbage mixture to a large glass jar or other container. Pack the cabbage into the jar, pressing down firmly as you go and leaving about 1 inch of head space at the top of the jar. Pour any liquid left in the bowl into the jar. Seal the jar tightly and set it aside at room temperature for 2 days.

5 Check the kimchee once a day, pressing down on the vegetables with a spoon to keep them submerged in liquid. After 2 days, refrigerate the kimchee. It will be ready to serve in 4 days and can be kept refrigerated for up to 2 weeks.

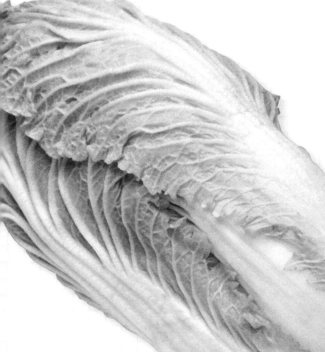

SOUTHWEST RELISH

4 ears corn

2 tablespoons vegetable oil

1 white onion, sliced

¼ cup finely chopped fresh cilantro

¼ cup finely chopped fresh parsley

1 red bell pepper, diced

1 14-ounce can of black beans, rinsed and drained

1 jalapeño, seeded and finely chopped

Kosher salt to taste

Makes 3 cups A side dish from the Moonshine Patio Bar & Grill in Austin, Texas, gave me the idea for this spicy relish that is as much at home on the side of the plate as it is on its own. I've made succotash using roasted corn and edamame, but to my taste, this is an even better way to use roasted fresh corn. Roasting it on the cob and letting it get a little bit of char greatly enhances the flavor of the corn and adds smoky notes. Try this as a condiment on a burger.

1 Preheat the oven to 450°F.

2 Peel back the corn husks, keeping them attached, and remove the silk. Re-cover the corn with the husks and microwave on high until fully cooked, about 6 minutes.

3 Being careful of the steam, peel back the husks to form a long handle around the stem of each ear. Place the corn directly on the oven rack and roast until toasted with a few black spots, turning a few times, 2 to 3 minutes per side. Remove the corn from the oven and set aside to cool.

4 In a skillet set over medium-low heat, heat the oil and cook the onion for about 5 minutes, until the slices are soft and caramelized.

5 In a large bowl, hold an ear of corn by its "handle" and slide a knife down the cob to cut off the kernels. Repeat with the remaining ears of corn. Toss in the cooked onions and the remaining ingredients, and stir to combine. Season to taste and serve.

SWEETS

WHEN PEOPLE ASK ME, "ARE YOU

a sweet person or a savory person?" my response is usually the too-clever-by-half "Depends on who you ask!" The truth is, though I do tend to fall on the savory side of the spectrum, even for me, nothing caps a great meal quite like a cup of coffee and a well-crafted sweet treat. The heights of ecstasy a chocolate dessert can evoke within me are of near-religious proportions, and my mom has opened my eyes to the merits of a sweet fruit dessert like a cobbler or a crumble. Whether you veer toward creamy, salty peanut butter or rich, velvety chocolate, sweet caramel, or cool custardy ice cream or pudding, dessert is the coda, the grand finale of the symphony that is a well-constructed menu.

That's why you should always have a few easy go-to recipes to round out a special meal or celebrate a special occasion without resorting to something store-bought (though components of a homemade dish certainly can be). And believe me, it's worth that final effort. When *every* element of your meal is straight up tasty, from start to finish, because you've made everything from the sauces to the salads, steaks, and s'mores, you're going to love your newfound culinary badassery . . . and realize how truly sweet it is knowing you've served something that came from your very own kitchen, your very own hands, and your very own heart.

S'MORES CUPS

Makes 12 cups I've taken the campfire favorite to the next level here. You can eat these while everything is still melty and hot, or you can let the cups cool and server them warm or at room temperature.

3 tablespoons unsalted butter, melted, divided

4 sheets of phyllo dough, thawed

¼ cup graham cracker crumbs, divided

1½ ounces milk chocolate, chopped

1 tablespoon chocolate syrup, approximately

⅓ cup mini marshmallows

1 Preheat the oven to 350°F. Grease a 12-cup mini-muffin tin with 1 tablespoon of the melted butter.

2 Lay one sheet of phyllo dough on a clean cutting board. Brush the sheet with a little of the melted butter, dust with some of the graham cracker crumbs, and place another sheet of phyllo over it. Repeat until you have 4 layers, and finish by buttering the top layer.

3 Cut the phyllo into 3½ x 3-inch squares (about the size of the muffin cups) by cutting the long side in quarters and the short side in thirds. Press the phyllo squares into the tin to line the muffin cups with dough.

4 Divide the chocolate among the cups. Top each cup with about ½ teaspoon graham cracker crumbs and about ¼ teaspoon chocolate syrup. Top each with three mini marshmallows. Fold the corners of dough inward over each cup. Brush the edges with the remaining melted butter.

5 Bake the cups until the dough is golden brown and the chocolate is mostly melted, about 9 minutes.

I created the three recipes that follow for a Halloween appearance on the *Today* show. The theme was the royal wedding. Giada De Laurentiis showed up dressed as Katy Perry in the *California Gurls* video, and I, because it was the only costume from the costume shop that fit, was done up as Rhett Butler. Clearly this was not going to be a conventional holiday celebration, so I wanted to have recipes that were a bit surprising. From easy stuff that you can make with kids, like the broken-candy ice cream sandwich, to a variation on salted caramel cheesecake, these recipes will definitely please even your littlest Halloween fans and can be enjoyed year-round.

CHOCOLATE MINT BLIZZARD SHAKE

Makes 1 shake (about 10 ounces)

4 to 6 Peppermint Patties, broken into pieces (or 1 4.75-ounce box of Junior Mints), plus more for garnish

¾ to 1 cup whole milk

Splash of pure vanilla extract

A few ice cubes

Combine all the ingredients in a blender and blend until smooth. Pour into a tall glass and garnish with extra crumbled patties or whole Junior Mints.

BROKEN-CANDY ICE CREAM SANDWICH

1 whole Hershey's Krackel or Nestlé Crunch bar, or a 1.69-ounce bag of plain M&M's

2 large chocolate chip cookies

1 large scoop of vanilla ice cream, slightly softened

Makes 1 sandwich Chocolate chip cookies and vanilla ice cream are safe choices here, but you can really use any kind of cookie or ice cream filling that you like. Go crazy!

1 Put the candy in a sealable plastic bag and roll over it with a rolling pin to break the candies into small chunks. (You can also place the bag underneath a heavy cutting board and press down on the board to achieve the same result.) Pour the broken bits onto a plate.

2 Put the scoop of ice cream on the top of one cookie, top with the second cookie and press until the ice cream is almost squeezing out the sides. Roll the sandwich like a wheel in the broken candy to completely cover the exposed surface of the ice cream. Wrap the sandwich in plastic wrap and freeze until hardened.

ICE CREAM SANDWICHES

Ice cream sandwiches are one of my favorite desserts. They're super easy—ice cream sandwiched between two cookies—but you can make any number of variations, rolling the ice cream edges in complementary extras. Here are some great options:

Chocolate Chip Cookies, Mint Chocolate Chip Ice Cream, Rolled in Broken Candy Canes and Chocolate Sauce.

Butter Cookies, Bourbon Vanilla Ice Cream, Rolled in Crushed Pecans and Maple Syrup.

Gingersnaps, Chocolate Ice Cream, Rolled in Chili Powder–Toasted Pumpkin Seeds and Powdered Ginger

Sugar Cookies, Strawberry Ice Cream, Rolled in Fresh-Torn Mint and Basil and Chocolate Sauce.

OH, HELL YES CHEESECAKE

Makes 1 8½-inch cheesecake Yet another inspired way to use up those Halloween leftovers, with Kit Kat, Butterfinger, and caramel candies all adding their distinctive sweet notes to the proceedings.

FOR THE CRUST

5½ tablespoons butter

6 Kit Kat milk chocolate wafer bar sticks, frozen

1 cup graham cracker crumbs

⅓ cup sugar

Pinch of salt

FOR THE FILLING

4 ounces Butterfinger candy, frozen

3 8-ounce packages of cream cheese, softened

1¼ cups sugar

4 tablespoons all-purpose flour

5 large eggs, beaten

3 egg yolks, beaten

1 teaspoon pure vanilla extract

TO FINISH

16 caramels, such as Brach's Milk Maid Caramels

Sea salt to taste

1 Make the crust: Grease a 9-inch springform pan with 1 tablespoon of the butter. In a small saucepan, melt the remaining butter over low heat. Place the Kit Kats in a food processor and chop until they are reduced to crumbs. Transfer to a large bowl and add the graham cracker crumbs, melted butter, sugar, and salt. Combine well. Press the mixture into the bottom of the prepared pan (about ¼ inch thick), and place it in the refrigerator to chill.

2 Make the filling: Place the Butterfinger candy in the food processor and chop until it is reduced to crumbs. Transfer to a large bowl or the bowl of a stand mixer. Add the cream cheese, sugar, flour, eggs, egg yolks, and vanilla to the bowl and mix with a hand mixer or stand mixer until well combined. Cover the bowl and place it in the refrigerator to chill for at least an hour.

3 Preheat the oven to 350°F.

4 Place the chilled crust on a rimmed baking sheet. Pour in the filling. Bake for 12 minutes, then lower the heat to 200°F and cook for 1 hour, until the filling is just set and browned. Remove the cheesecake from the oven, cool to room temperature, about 20 to 30 minutes, then cover it loosely and refrigerate for at least 6 hours.

5 To finish: Remove the chilled cheesecake from the refrigerator approximately 10 minutes before serving. Put the caramels in a small microwave-safe bowl and add about 1 inch of water. Microwave, uncovered, on high until the caramels are melted, about 90 seconds. Stir well. Drizzle the melted caramel over the cheesecake. Sprinkle with sea salt. Serve when the cake is just slightly cooler than room temperature.

MIXED BERRY CLAFOUTI

1 tablespoon unsalted butter

1½ cups whole milk

⅓ cup sugar

3 eggs

Freshly grated zest of 1 lemon

½ cup all-purpose flour

1 cup fresh sweet cherries, pitted

1 cup fresh blueberries

1 cup fresh raspberries

Confectioners' sugar, for garnish

Serves 6 I learned a version of this dish while on my very first professional acting job out of drama school. There I was, a formerly dirt-poor grad student, in a beautiful DC apartment with a view of the Potomac and a huge kitchen. I had money in my pocket, a place to experiment, and a friend whose wife had just written some major cookbooks for major restaurants like The Palm. Clafouti was my pal's favorite dish, and when his wife gave me the recipe, handwritten on a sheet of paper ripped from a spiral notebook, she called it "Casey's Clafouti." To me it was a cross between a flan and a custard and more impressive than any dish I had ever made before, dessert-wise. I still love it. Feel free to substitute the berries you like best or whatever is in season.

1 Preheat the oven to 350°F. Grease a 9-inch round baking dish with the butter.

2 In the bowl of a standing mixer, combine the milk, sugar, eggs, lemon zest, and flour. Beat on low speed to make a thin batter.

3 Pour in half of the batter. Place the dish in the oven and bake until the batter begins to set but isn't baked through, about 8 minutes.

4 Scatter the cherries, blueberries, and raspberries over the batter. Pour the remaining batter over the fruit. Return to the oven and bake until the clafouti is browned, about 20 minutes. It is finished when you insert a butter knife and it comes out clean.

5 Sprinkle the clafouti with confectioners' sugar and serve warm.

SALTED CARAMEL CANDY APPLE TARTS

4 large Granny Smith apples, cored and sliced

1 tablespoon ground cinnamon

1 or 2 pinches of ground nutmeg

14 Brach's Milk Maid Caramels

1 package of refrigerated pie crust

Sea salt to taste

1 tablespoon unsalted butter, melted

Makes 6 tarts Three facts you should know about my mom: she is highly awesome, she is a phenomenal cook, and she loves fruit desserts. So in part this dessert is a tribute to her, but also to my late father. Not too far from where I grew up in Brooklyn was an amusement park called Nellie Bly, where he often took me. This was where I had my very first candy apple, and subsequently my very first toothache and red, sticky face. While I wasn't such a big fan of the translucent titanium-red coating on the conventional candy apple, I did really appreciate the sweet, sticky coating of caramel apples. I wanted to combine that crunchy hard shell with the gooeyness we encounter once we start eating the apple.

1 Preheat the oven to 350°F.

2 Spread the apple slices in an oven-safe baking dish large enough to hold them without touching. Season with the cinnamon and nutmeg. Bake until soft, but not mushy, about 5 minutes.

3 Put the caramels in a glass dish and add about 1 inch of water. Microwave, uncovered, on high, stirring occasionally, until completely melted, about 90 seconds.

4 Dip 6 of the apple slices into the hot caramel. Put the dipped slices on a plate and refrigerate them until the caramel is set.

5 Unfold the pie crust and roll it into a rectangle. Cut the dough into 6 squares and use them to line 6 individual pie or tart pans, or 6-ounce ramekins, cutting off the excess.

6 Divide the plain baked apple slices among the pie shells. Drizzle with the caramel and season with sea salt. Brush the edges of the pie crusts with the melted butter.

7 Bake the tarts for 20 to 25 minutes, until the pie pastry is golden. Serve warm, topping each tart with a hard candy apple slice.

TART FRUIT POPS

½ cup fresh raspberries

2 cups lemonade (use a
natural one, or one as
lightly sweetened as
possible)

6 wooden ice-pop sticks

Makes 6 pops This is another super-easy but delicious dessert. Kids will love the pops, and adults could use them as tasty cocktail stirrers. The pops are just fresh fruit mixed with fruit juice and frozen onto a stick. If you have an ice-pop mold, it's a no-brainer. If not, all you need is an ice cube tray and wooden sticks. You can make these pops with all kinds of fruits, but more solid fruits (like pineapple) work better than soft ones (mango). Here are some of my other favorite flavor combinations:

PINEAPPLE AND RED GRAPE JUICE
CANNED (OR FRESH, BUT FIRM) PEACHES AND APPLE JUICE
STRAWBERRIES AND LIMEADE

Fill your ice-pop mold with berries, then add the lemonade. Insert the handles and freeze according to the manufacturer's instructions. Alternatively, fill an ice cube tray with the raspberries and cover with the lemonade. Freeze until the fruit is almost firm, about 30 minutes. Insert the sticks and return to the freezer until completely solid.

MOLE CHOCOLATE PUDDING
with TOASTED PUMPKIN SEEDS
and FRESH WHIPPED VANILLA CREAM

½ cup raw unshelled, unsalted pumpkin seeds

1 dried ancho chile, stemmed, seeded, and chopped

2 cups whole milk

2 teaspoons finely ground coffee

1 teaspoon cinnamon

⅓ cup sugar, plus
  1 tablespoon for the whipped cream

⅓ cup unsweetened cocoa

2 tablespoons cornstarch

2 large eggs, beaten

3 ounces (70% cocoa) bittersweet chocolate, finely chopped

1 cup very cold heavy cream

1 teaspoon pure vanilla extract

Serves 6 to 8 Mole, the sensual blend of chiles and chocolate that originated in the Mexican region of Oaxaca, is traditionally used as a sauce, usually for simmering. I have heard that the sensation of tasting a properly made mole is biochemically equivalent to the experience of love. No wonder people love to experiment with it! I've had mole in gelato, as a drizzle over tacos, and, in this case, in a pudding. It has those wonderfully balanced notes of spicy, sweet, fruity, and nutty. Kind of like life.

1 In a saucepan set over medium heat, toast the pumpkin seeds for about 1 minute. Remove the seeds from the heat and place them on a plate. Add the chile pieces to the saucepan and toast for about 1 minute.

2 Pour the milk over the chile pieces and bring it to a simmer. Cover the pan, remove it from the heat, and let the chile-milk mixture steep for 20 minutes. Stir in the coffee and cinnamon until completely dissolved. Transfer the mixture to a bowl, remove the chile pieces, and let the liquid cool to room temperature.

3 In a medium bowl, combine ⅓ cup of the sugar with the cocoa and the cornstarch. Pour in about ½ cup of the milk mixture and whisk to make a smooth paste. Slowly whisk in the rest of the milk. Return the contents of the bowl to the saucepan used for the milk-chile-coffee mixture.

4 Heat this mixture over medium heat, stirring occasionally, until it begins to bubble around the edges. Reduce the heat to low and stir constantly for 2 minutes, or until the mixture has thickened. Remove the pan from the heat.

5 *Very slowly*, pour about 1 cup of the hot mixture over the beaten eggs in their bowl, whisking constantly. (Pour *slowly*, or the eggs will scramble). Whisk to fully combine, and then pour the egg mixture back into the saucepan with the rest of the hot milk mixture. Return the pan to medium heat and whisk until all the ingredients are thoroughly combined, about 1 minute.

6 Remove the saucepan from the heat. Add the chopped chocolate and whisk until smooth.

7 Transfer the pudding to a clean bowl. Cover it with plastic wrap, making sure the plastic wrap is directly on the surface of the pudding to prevent a skin from forming. Place the bowl in the refrigerator until cool, at least 1 hour.

8 In a large bowl, combine the cream, the remaining 2 tablespoons of sugar, and the vanilla. Whip until medium peaks form, about 2 minutes. Refrigerate until ready to serve.

9 Top the chilled pudding with the whipped cream and sprinkle the toasted pumpkin seeds on top.

WIN-THE-BAKE-SALE CHOCOLATE CAKE

Makes 1 9-inch double-layer cake Couldn't be easier and couldn't be more chocolaty and delicious. What more can you ask for, really? This is all about ease and a guaranteed tasty result. Betty Crocker has done a lot of the heavy lifting here, and the one major difference is appropriated from Portillo's in Chicago, and that would be the addition of mayonnaise for extra rich, creamy fluffiness. Before you turn up your nose, remember this: mayonnaise is only oil and eggs. You're gonna be okay. Trust me.

1 box of Betty Crocker SuperMoist Butter Recipe Chocolate Cake Mix

3 large eggs

½ cup Hellmann's Light Mayonnaise

1 can of store-bought chocolate frosting

1 Preheat the oven to 350°F. Grease two 9-inch round cake pans with cooking spray.

2 In a large bowl, whisk together the cake mix, eggs, 1 cup of cold water, and the mayonnaise.

3 Pour the mixture into the greased cake pans and spread with a spatula to smooth. Bake according to package instructions. When done, remove the pans from the oven and place them on wire racks to cool completely.

4 Invert one of the cake layers onto a plate. Using a rubber spatula, spread a thick layer of frosting over the top. Carefully invert the other cake layer on top and spread the top and sides with the remaining frosting.

A HISTORY OF CHOCOLATE IN RHYME

We sample great tastes from the time of our birth
Though we have not quite learned how to talk yet.
And one of the greatest on all planet earth,
Is undeniably chocolate.

We love it as ice cream, we love it as cake,
That we love it is not a mystery.
But how many of us know where it came from?
Who really knows dear chocolate's history?

So let's go back in time, with the aid of a rhyme,
And take a chocolaty trip.
To appreciate this amazing food great,
Skip the cookie, let's look at the chip.

As far as we know, where we first need to go,
Is Mesoamerica 1900 BC
Where the Olmec and Maya, and also Mokaya,
Would eat cacao beans right off of the tree.

They thought that these pods were gifts from the gods,
And they ground them up into a drink.
Mixed with chiles and cornmeal, fermented and frothy
Not my bag—but what do you think?

When the Aztecs took power, they grew no cacao flowers,
But imported them, and took them as tax.
One hundred cacao beans could buy you a turkey,
I'm not making it up—those are facts!

The Aztecs began drinking their chocolate cold,
After meals or to boost their libido.
Moctezuma even included it in soldiers' rations,
Admit it, that is kind of neato.

Then the Spanish came over, and Hernán Cortés,
Conquered the Aztecs and brought chocolate to Spain.
They added sugar and honey to keep it from tasting too funny,
And they also gave chocolate its name.

There are so many theories of how chocolate got named,
Are the roots Nahuatl, Aztec, or Mayan?
"Cacao drink," "bitter water" are two believed meanings,
Someone's right and someone is lyin'!

Chocolate spread throughout Europe, to the English, French, Dutch
Amidst the time of Industrial Revolution,
It was loved everywhere, so there was some good there
And not just a lot of pollution.

When Van Houten (that's Coenraad) added alkaline salts,
The chocolate became much less bitter.
He removed half the cacao butter with his patented press,
Imagine if he'd been a quitter!

While I know you think that, in removing the fat,
He committed a big flavor no-no.
But it kept quality great, it was cheaper to make,
And this was soon known as "Dutch Cocoa."

Now while many nations contribute to our infatuation,
Chocolate fans: you surely know this.
Many countries have shaped the chocolate we love,
But none quite as much as the Swiss.

Milk chocolate was made by Daniel Peter,
Using powdered milk from Henri Nestlé.
And then Rodolphe Lindt left *his* chocolate imprint,
Making it creamy, not crumbly and messy.

In the late nineteenth century, the demand for chocolate,
Went from huge to extraordinary.
Two names would emerge, to deal with this surge,
One was Hershey, the other Cadbury.

And now chocolate's everywhere, in every meal,
It is versatile; it is all-seasonal.
You can get many brands from across many lands
From the popular to the artisanal.

Mixed with quinoa, or sea salt, or caramel-filled,
With chiles or just served up plain,
However you eat it, once you taste chocolate,
Your life will not be quite the same.

CHALLAH BREAD PUDDIN'
with BOURBON SAUCE

Unsalted butter, to grease the muffin tin

3 tablespoons heavy cream

½ cup whole milk

2 teaspoons bourbon

2 large eggs, beaten

3 tablespoons (packed) light brown sugar

½ teaspoon pure vanilla extract

¼ teaspoon ground cinnamon

¼ teaspoon freshly grated nutmeg

Pinch of kosher salt

1¼ cups cubed challah or egg bread rolls

Confectioners' sugar, for garnish

Bourbon Sauce (recipe follows)

Serves 4 Anyone who knows me knows how much I love New Orleans, not to mention the savory dishes that the Big Easy is known for: jambalaya, gumbo, redfish, crawfish. But too often the amazing desserts to be had there are overlooked. King cake, a circular vanilla-cinnamon cake iced in the gold, green, and purple of Mardi Gras, with a tiny plastic baby hidden somewhere within the flaky pastry, has its fans, and we cannot forget the beignet—pieces of exquisite fried sugary love served up at Cafe Du Monde on Decatur Street—but do you know about revered treats like snowballs and doberge cake? Probably not. But if there's a dessert that visitors and natives alike seem to agree upon it is good old-fashioned bread pudding. With the natural egginess of Jewish challah bread and a little bit of vanilla, the effect is not unlike a somewhat soggier king cake. And the bourbon sauce is pure New Orleans. By the way, if you're looking for great bread pudding in New Orleans, you have to try the Parkway Bakery.

1 Grease 4 muffin cups with the butter and set aside.

2 In a large bowl, stir together the heavy cream, milk, bourbon, eggs, brown sugar, vanilla, cinnamon, nutmeg, and salt. Stir in the bread cubes. Allow the mixture to sit at room temperature, stirring occasionally, until the bread is soggy, about 30 minutes.

3 Preheat the oven to 350°F. Evenly divide the bread mixture among the buttered muffin cups and bake until the centers of the bread puddings are set, approximately 30 minutes.

4 Garnish with confectioners' sugar and serve the pudding while still warm. Spoon the bourbon sauce over the top (or serve it in a container on the side).

RECIPE CONTINUES

BOURBON SAUCE

Makes ⅔ cup

½ cup heavy cream

3 tablespoons whole milk

3 tablespoons sugar

1 teaspoon cornstarch

1 tablespoon bourbon, divided

Pinch of salt

1 tablespoon unsalted butter

1　In a small pot set over medium heat, combine the cream, milk, and sugar. Whisk the mixture together until the sugar is dissolved.

2　In a small mixing bowl, whisk the cornstarch and ½ tablespoon of the bourbon to blend and make a slurry. Pour the slurry into the cream mixture and bring it to a boil.

3　Once the sauce begins to boil, reduce the heat to a gentle simmer and cook, stirring occasionally, for 5 minutes or until the sauce no longer tastes like cornstarch.

4　Remove the sauce from the heat, add the salt, and stir in the butter and the remaining ½ tablespoon of bourbon. Stir until the butter is melted and well incorporated.

5　Serve warm. (The leftover sauce can be kept, covered and refrigerated, for up to a week.)

NUTTY CHOCOLATE CRUNCH BITES

Makes about 4 cups I sometimes call these haystacks, but my less mature buddies call them "tasty turds," both because of their appearance and because my friends can sometimes say some stupid stuff. Yes, they do look like chocolate clumps of madness. Yes, they taste freaking delicious, are completely addictive, and are easy to make. In fact, with a description like that—amazing, easy to make in the home, and addictive—maybe we could call them Heisenberg peanut chews? Here are two different variations, both equally appealing.

VERSION 1

1 Break the chocolate up and place it in a medium microwave-safe bowl. Microwave on high in 10-second increments, stirring after each, until the chocolate is melted.

2 Stir in the chow mein noodles and cereal and mix until combined.

3 Line a baking tray with wax paper. Place tablespoon-size dollops of the chocolate-crunch mixture on the tray and refrigerate until hardened, about 2 hours. Transfer to a covered container and store at room temperature for up to 1 week, or as long as they last.

VERSION 2

1 Line a large plate with wax paper. Using a melon baller or two spoons, make small balls of peanut butter and place them on the prepared plate. Refrigerate until hard but still sticky, about 30 minutes.

2 Combine the chopped chocolate and crumbled chow mein noodles on a second plate. Roll the peanut butter balls in the mixture to coat, then refrigerate again until firm, another 30 minutes. Transfer to a covered container and store in the refrigerator for up to 1 week.

8 ounces of your favorite chocolate (semi-sweet, milk, dark)

1 cup dried chow mein noodles, crumbled

1 cup of your favorite cereal

2 cups smooth peanut butter (not organic or the oil will separate)

1 1.55-ounce milk chocolate bar, finely chopped

1 cup dried chow mein noodles, crumbled

ACKNOWLEDGMENTS

I NEVER THOUGHT I'D WRITE A COOKBOOK.

I never thought I could. And the truth is, I can't. I can come up with kick-ass recipes. I can create big flavor bombs to explode all up in your mouth. I can remember and combine ingredients from a dish I had in Hiroshima, Japan, four years ago, with a cooking technique I learned in a corrugated steel shack in South Carolina. That I can do. But write a real, actual cookbook? No. That I cannot do. At the very least, I could not do it alone.

Michael Psaltis and everyone on his team at the CEA have gone above and beyond (as they always do) to research recipes, fine-tune measurements, and even meticulously test the recipes before this book was close to hitting shelves. Mike has always had faith in me even when I've lost it in myself and he is the exact guy you want on your team, in your foxhole, and in your kitchen. He's been one of the single, most positive forces in my culinary career and, truth be told, my career as a whole thus far, and I love him. This book could not exist without him.

Pam Krauss has been my editor since my first book, and she instilled both fear and great respect in me from our first meeting. She *is* the culinary world; she *is* the world of pop culture; she is ridiculously literate, terrifyingly intelligent, and, thankfully, relentlessly efficient and seems to be biologically incapable of sugar-coating anything. As any author or creative professional will tell you, such people are worth their weight in gold. Pam is no different. She shoots from the hip, aims for the heart, and never expects of others a work ethic she does not put forth herself. She is the example; she is the judge I answer to. She is Yoda. She is Darth. She is awesome.

Eileen Stringer is the reason I am pretty much able to do anything. I have no assistant. I have no right-hand man. I have no secretary. I do, however, have an unbelievable manager who has had faith in me since I was an understudy at the Mark Taper forum. She functions in all those capacities I have named, as well as surrogate mom, erstwhile psychotherapist, relationship coach, social media advisor, crisis management coordinator, and beloved friend. She has kept me on track and my eyes on the prize. I no longer seek to deliver good product for my manager, I just always want Eileen to be proud of me. She's the glue that holds the house together.

Teal Cannaday, my publicist, is a gem. I've not always made things super easy for her, and I'm not proud of that. But she has always handled awkward PR stuff with grace and tact that I did not think was possible in the adverse situations she comes across. She has kept the whole media thing fun, positive, focused, and effective, and she really has had my back and been the buffer many a time when the slings and arrows of outrageous fortune and notoriety have been more aggressive than others. She gives me gravity and levity—miraculously at the same time—while looking absolutely amazing.

Evan Sung and his whole team have taken recipes from my cluttered Brooklyn kitchen and elevated them, through his gorgeous photos, to works of absolute beauty, fun, joy, and hunger-inducing deliciousness. He is endlessly creative, has the patience of a saint, and is as ready with a laugh as he is to correct an f-stop. He is the rare master artist who is still open to dialogue and collaboration, and this book would be a bland affair without his considerable gifts and those of his team.

Finally, I would like to thank Suzanne Lenzer and her team for cooking my dishes and making many of them prettier than I ever did or could. To see true culinary craftsmen, poring over recipes that came from my travels or peripatetic fever dreams across my taste buds, and devoting hours to style them, perfect them as if they were their own, is such a humbling sight. My sincere thanks to all of you for your constant generosity and the hours of skilled labor you put into *Straight Up Tasty*. I am indebted to you all.

To my agents Ben Simone, Scott Wachs, Amir Shakhalili, Jon Rosen, and Jeff Googel at WME: you have allowed me the chance to play this game on the highest level and you have stood by my side and believed in me when others have not. Thank you for the hours spent in negotiations and phone calls, on planes, and in meeting rooms, all so I can have the opportunities that have resulted in the creation of these recipes and this book. My thanks to you all.

To Matt Sharp, Dan Adler, Bob Larson, Bonnie Biggs, Dan Kornfeld, Tony Biancosino, Cat Pappas, and my whole crew from Sharp Entertainment and the shows we've done together for the past seven years: You are my family, my travel companions, my colleagues, my comrades in arms, my crew, my clique, my team, and my friends. We have taken many of these journeys together and sampled many of the dishes that inspired these recipes. I love you guys with all of my heart, and I look forward to our next adventures.

To my incredible fans, who believed in an unknown guy and his capacity to not only eat a five-pound burrito but believed that he was capable of doing so much more: You have been with me since day one in good times and bad, and I will always strive to be worthy of you and your support. You'll never know how truly grateful I am.

Finally, my family—especially my beautiful mother, my lovely stepmother, my amazing grandma, and my late, great Aunt Anne: You have always been there for me, through thick and thin, and you are the finest home cooks I have ever known. You've taught me and fed me, in and out of the kitchen. You've made my life delicious in ways far beyond those of food. You are a gift, you are my heart, and everything I do is for you guys.

Thank You.

ADAM RICHMAN
BROOKLYN, NEW YORK

INDEX

Note: Page references in *italics* indicate photographs.

S

ADDITIONAL PHOTOGRAPHY CREDITS